Civilian Post-Deployment Reintegration

A Review and Analysis of Practices Across U.S. Federal Agencies

MOLLY DUNIGAN, KRISTIE L. GORE, KATHERINE L. KIDDER,
MICHAEL SCHWILLE, SAMANTHA CHERNEY, JAMES SLADDEN

RAND
CORPORATION

For more information on this publication, visit www.rand.org/t/RR3220

Library of Congress Cataloging-in-Publication Data is available for this publication.
ISBN: 978-1-9774-0424-4

Published by the RAND Corporation, Santa Monica, Calif.

Cover design by Rick Penn-Kraus;
saluting soldier: MariaArefyeva/Getty Images/iStockphoto;
man at airport: ViewApart/Getty Images/iStockphoto

Preface

The United States has deployed an unprecedented number of U.S. federal government civilians to theaters of conflict over the past two decades to perform a wide variety of tasks, from administrative support to development assistance and diplomatic functions. As more civilians have deployed, increasing numbers have been exposed to high-threat environments and high levels of stress. Studies of civilians, both government-employed and contractors, deployed to theaters of conflict over the past two decades indicate that combat exposure and related stressors correlate with significant levels of deployment-related health conditions for this population. Anecdotal evidence further confirms that deployed civilians face similar deployment-related challenges as those experienced by military personnel, in terms of health conditions and family challenges associated with lengthy deployments. Based on this prior work and evidence, there is likely a need for civilian post-deployment reintegration support.

However, until now, a descriptive account of the specific policies, processes, tools, and outputs associated with reintegration for deployed civilians has been lacking. The U.S. military has extensively studied and categorized many post-deployment issues and devoted considerable funding to the provision of services for U.S. Department of Defense (DoD) personnel. By comparison, it appears that there is a relative dearth of post-deployment services available to civilian deployees. This report documents the results of an exploratory research endeavor to identify current activities, policies, and procedures that both DoD and non-DoD federal agencies can use to reintegrate a civilian following a domestic or overseas deployment to a high-threat environment.

This research should be of interest to policymakers, managers, and personnel in federal agencies that routinely deploy civilian personnel domestically or internationally to high-threat or high-stress environments. It should also prove useful for researchers and decision-makers who are interested in developing methods and strategies to more effectively and efficiently reintegrate civilians following a deployment.

RAND Ventures

RAND is a research organization that develops solutions to public policy challenges to help make communities throughout the world safer and more secure, healthier and more prosperous. RAND is nonprofit, nonpartisan, and committed to the public interest.

RAND Ventures is a vehicle for investing in policy solutions. Philanthropic contributions support our ability to take the long view, tackle tough and often-controversial topics, and share our findings in innovative and compelling ways. RAND's research findings and recommendations are based on data and evidence, and therefore do not necessarily reflect the policy preferences or interests of its clients, donors, or supporters.

Funding for this venture was made possible by the independent research and development provisions of RAND's contracts for the operation of its U.S. Department of Defense federally funded research and development centers.

Support for this project is also provided, in part, by the income earned on client-funded research and from other donors. For more information about RAND Ventures, visit www.rand.org/giving/ventures.

Contents

Figures and Tables

Figures

Tables

Summary

In the conflicts in Iraq and Afghanistan over the past two decades, the United States has deployed an unprecedented number of U.S. government civilians to perform a wide variety of tasks. Meanwhile, numerous federal agencies deploy civilian personnel as needed to high-threat environments and high levels of stress that are not active theaters of war to conduct various activities from disaster relief to diplomatic concerns to drug enforcement.

Prior RAND Corporation research[1] focusing on the identification, sourcing, and readiness preparation of U.S. federal civilians for deployment recognized a post-deployment *decompression*[2] or *redeployment*, stage associated with the deployment of civilians from the U.S. interagency community. Considered in its most comprehensive sense, this post-deployment stage constitutes a variety of efforts to reintegrate deployees (and, ideally, their families) into civilian life following

---

1 Molly Dunigan, Michael Schwille, Susanne Sondergaard, Susan S. Sohler Everingham, and Todd Nichols, *Expeditionary Civilians: Creating a Viable Practice of Civilian Deployment Within the U.S. Interagency Community and Among Foreign Defense Organizations*, Santa Monica, Calif.: RAND Corporation, RR-1249-OSD, 2016; Molly Dunigan, Susan S. Sohler Everingham, Todd Nichols, Michael Schwille, and Susanne Sondergaard, *Expeditionary Civilians: Creating a Viable Practice of Department of Defense Civilian Deployment*, Santa Monica, Calif.: RAND Corporation, RR-975-OSD, 2016.

2 Dunigan, Everingham, et al. (2016) used the terminology *decompression* for the entire post-deployment reintegration process. During the course of this research, we refined the term to be only one of several specific programs. For the remainder of this report, the term decompression will be used in this context and will not be used to represent the entire post-deployment reintegration process.

a deployment.[3] Yet, until now, a descriptive account of the specific policies, processes, tools, and outputs associated with this post-deployment reintegration stage of civilian deployment has been lacking, because this stage of civilian deployment has not yet been assessed across organizations of interest. Markedly absent from the literature on post-deployment programs and activities, therefore, is a substantive discussion or evaluation of redeployment practices for these federal civilian deployees, many of whom are in areas where they have a similar likelihood of exposure to combat and related stressors as experienced by deployed U.S. troops.

Therefore, this report is an important step toward exploring the post-deployment practices of a broad array of U.S. federal agencies with regard to their civilian deployees. To do so, the research team for this study aimed to answer three related research questions:

1. What are the current post-deployment reintegration practices for U.S. federal civilian deployees?
2. How do civilian post-deployment reintegration activities, programs, and goals vary across non-DoD federal organizations and in relation to DoD?
3. What promising practices can be identified to ensure that civilians receive the support they need to reintegrate into civilian life after deployment?

The scope of this study is limited in several respects. This research focuses specifically on DoD and non-DoD civilian deployment, considering U.S. service member reintegration practices as a comparative case through which to derive lessons regarding potentially promising practices for civilian deployment. This is an exploratory study, limited to post-deployment practices for reintegration; therefore, the findings

---

[3] Reintegration is composed of activities, programs, and practices designed to provide support to service members and civilians upon return from a deployment. We define *reintegration* as the resumption of age, gender, and culturally appropriate roles in the family, community, and workplace, and the process of transitioning back into personal and organizational roles following deployment. See the glossary in Appendix A for a full description of post-deployment reintegration.

should be considered only as an illustrative attempt at demonstrating the scope and scale of relevant issues associated with such practices, programs, and activities, and highlighting relevant areas for future research.

Approach

The research approach combined a limited literature review and stakeholder interviews. The literature review relied on open-source publications from both academic and government sources to understand the range of existing DoD, service-specific, and civilian post-deployment reintegration activities, practices, and programs. The research team considered DoD and service-specific military reintegration practices as a baseline from which to compare and potentially draw lessons learned to inform civilian post-deployment reintegration efforts. The interview sample included deployees, direct line managers of people deployed, human resources personnel, and individuals in medical support and organizational management positions in both DoD and non-DoD federal agencies.

Promising Practices from DoD and Service-Specific Military Reintegration Experiences

Substantial programmatic efforts to prepare service members for combat deployments and to support them in a way that mitigates post-deployment impairment exist, but the research remains inconclusive on the effectiveness of these programs. Table S.1 describes types of reintegration practices. Psychological preparation, in the form of resilience-building, education, and peer support, makes up the largest proportion of programs to support post-deployment reintegration. Establishing evidentiary support is methodologically challenging because of the need to randomize people to control interventions, potentially withholding helpful services, or identifying matched samples on demographics and types of combat exposure and circumstances. Neverthe-

Table S.1
Categories of Reintegration Activity

Activity	Examples
Administrative outprocessing	Checklists, turning in equipment, update forms, and final paycheck
Health assessments	Post-deployment health assessments and medical checks
Decompression programs	Third location decompression rest and psychoeducation
Post-deployment leave	Administrative or regular leave
Incentives and recognition	Diplomate pay (or hazard pay), awards, and "welcome home" events
Workplace reintegration	Policies to protect office space and efforts to support a return to work
Community and family reintegration	Benefits assistance, family reunion activities, and education
Post-trauma practices	Stress management and psychotherapy
Personnel tracking	Monitoring personnel after return from a deployment
Individual mobilization augmentee assistance	Assigned case manager, educational websites on reintegration support programs

NOTE: These categories of reintegration activity were compiled from RAND analysis of post-deployment activities used by the DoD and from interviews with non-DoD civilian agencies.

less, these practices can still offer useful insights for developing post-deployment programs for U.S. federal agency civilian deployees.

Specific practices that U.S. federal agencies should consider for their civilian deployee populations include

- using personnel tracking of deployment characteristics (length, location, combat exposure) and health status
- requiring a post-deployment health assessment

- employing a case-management approach to tracking health status and matching available resources to individual needs
- researching to determine whether a designated period of rest following a combat deployment before resuming routine pre-deployment job duties facilitates reintegration
- ensuring that families of combat deployees are aware of and can access an extensive web of existing family and community support resources.

Although post-deployment reintegration practices from the military can serve as a source of guidance in developing programs for civilian deployees, federal agencies should pilot-test and evaluate the results of any such practices before adopting and adapting them.

U.S. Federal Agency Post-Deployment Reintegration Practices Vary Significantly Across Organizations

Table S.2 details the categorization of post-deployment activities among the organizations represented by the individuals interviewed for this study. The results illustrate that although all agencies engage in some post-deployment activities, there is little consistency across the federal agencies included in this study. Of the categories of reintegration activity considered here, interviewees most commonly reported experience with administrative outprocessing; interviewees also frequently reported experience with post-deployment leave as a type of reintegration practice.

Key Findings

Our research led to eight key findings.

1. *No reliable data exist, to date, on the size and scale of the issues facing individual civilian deployees, and more evidence-based research is needed.* Numerous studies look at pre-deployment

Table S.2
Breakdown of Formal Post-Deployment Reintegration Activities and Programs Across U.S. Federal Agencies

Organization	Administrative Outprocessing	Health Assessments	Decompression Activity	Post-Deployment Leave	Resiliency Training	Recognition	Reintegration Activities	Post-Trauma Practices	Personnel Tracking
Non-DoD Federal Civilians									
PSC									
DHS OIE									
U.S. Department of Commerce									
U.S. Department of Treasury									
Federal Air Marshals Service									
U.S. Forest Service									
DEA									

Table S.2—Continued

Organization	Administrative Outprocessing	Health Assessments	Decompression Activity	Post-Deployment Leave	Resiliency Training	Recognition	Reintegration Activities	Post-Trauma Practices	Personnel Tracking
U.S. Customs and Border Protection (CBP)									
USAID									
DoS									
DoD Civilians									
SIGAR									
Department of the Navy Expeditionary Civilian Program									
Department of the Air Force Expeditionary Civilian Program									

Table S.2—Continued

Organization	Administrative Outprocessing	Health Assessments	Decompression Activity	Post-Deployment Leave	Resiliency Training	Recognition	Reintegration Activities	Post-Trauma Practices	Personnel Tracking
DoD Expeditionary Civilian Program Office									
DoD Uniformed Service Members									
DoD Uniformed Service Members									

NOTE: Data reflects coded results of interviews and might be subject to some error because of interviewee perceptions. Because the sample size was relatively small, the results may not be entirely indicative of actual agency practices; in addition, only information for agencies where we had data were included. In cases where interview results were conflicting, coding favored inclusion of an activity in the results. DHS = U.S. Department of Homeland Security; DoS = U.S. Department of State; PSC = personal services contractors; OIE = Office of International Engagement; SIGAR = Special Inspector General for Afghanistan Reconstruction; USAID = U.S. Agency for International Development.

Yes

No

Some form of activity

Unknown

resilience training practices within DoD and foreign defense organizations and DoD post-deployment military reintegration policies and practices. However, little exists for the U.S. federal civilian workforce. To fully understand the scope and scale of the issues facing these civilian agencies, additional research is needed; to facilitate such research, more systematic data collection on this population and its needs is required.

2. *Although all agencies studied had a pre-deployment process, very few had a formal post-deployment process.* The majority of organizations have considered how best to prepare and deploy someone, and they have established policies, procedures, and practices to do so. However, in many cases, leadership in these organizations had given little or no consideration to how best to reintegrate personnel after a deployment. Policy and guidance governing the post-deployment process were insufficient, incomplete, or nonexistent in many cases. This was even true of individuals who had been deployed to high-risk countries and conflict areas.
3. *Civilian post-deployment reintegration concepts and practices vary across non-DoD federal agencies.* The DEA and USAID appear to provide the most comprehensive post-deployment reintegration processes. The DoS' Foreign Service Institute (FSI), meanwhile, is a leader in developing resilience training and outbriefings for individuals returning from high-stress assignments. Yet the research team did not find evidence of any common concept of post-deployment reintegration or standards of best practice for civilian reintegration across the interagency community.
4. *Individual deployments affect reintegration processes differently from unit deployments.* Although there are instances in which the military will deploy individual augmentees to a variety of headquarters and operational units, the military typically deploys personnel in units. When deploying within a unit structure, personnel generally go through a deployment and the ensuing redeployment process with their peers and as a group. Meanwhile, U.S. federal agency civilian personnel—who primarily

deploy as individuals—proceed through the reintegration processes individually or not at all.

5. *A civilian's employment category appears to affect his or her post-deployment reintegration options.* The provision of current civilian post-deployment reintegration concepts and practices varies widely across the federal government, with many depending upon the type of authority under which an individual is hired. Relevant categories of civilian employment across U.S. non-DoD federal agencies include civil service, foreign service, PSCs, reservists,[4] intermittent staff, government service employees, and local national personnel. Relevant categories of civilian deployment across DoD include civil service, PSC, and intermittent staff.
6. *PSCs typically receive no post-deployment reintegration support and are more difficult to track following the end of their contracts.* None of the PSCs interviewed had received any form of post-deployment support, and the research team was unable to find any examples of PSCs who had received post-deployment support. This raises the question of whether PSCs represent a hidden community with unseen issues within the wider community of deployed civilians.
7. *Civilian deployees must actively seek post-deployment reintegration assistance but often lack knowledge regarding the availability of reintegration activities.* Even in cases in which returned deployees were willing to ask for help, interviewees revealed that they did not know of the range of available services; therefore, they were unaware of what to request in terms of assistance and services.
8. *Efforts to seek reintegration assistance are stigmatized in some cases.* Some interviewees expressed concerns about the impact that asking for assistance might have on them or their careers, in the short or long term.

[4] Note that the term *reservist* here refers to non-DoD federal agency reservists, who deploy in civilian status. U.S. military reserve component members are not within the study's scope, because they deploy in uniformed status.

Recommendations

Our research indicates that these issues could be remedied through the adoption and effective implementation of the following recommendations:

1. *Individual agencies should mandate exit interviews during the redeployment process to assist organizations in tracking their deployees and to gain useful feedback on deployment-related issues.* This process could help future deployees understand the issues of deployment and be better prepared to confront them. It could also be used to collect best practices for the organization and could help to identify future policies and practices.
2. *Individual agencies should establish processes to effectively track civilians, including PSCs, following a deployment.* The ability to track returned personnel allows for easy medical follow-up at preidentified critical times for redeployed personnel, and to create a snapshot of deployed personnel in the workforce, the time they spent deployed, what they did, and how long ago they returned from a deployment.
3. *Individual agencies deploying civilians should raise awareness of existing policies, programs, and activities—and, in doing so, destigmatize efforts to seek help.* A comprehensive post-deployment reintegration policy could help to standardize the process and provide deployees with a reliable resource to reference. As part of such an effort, creation of an inclusive, step-by-step checklist of concrete steps to be taken upon redeployment would help deployees understand the redeployment process, availability of post-deployment reintegration programs, and relevant points of contact for assistance. Agencies should place special emphasis on destigmatizing access to these programs, particularly those aimed at improving mental health outcomes.
4. *Both DoD and non-DoD federal agencies should work together to consolidate and standardize civilian post-deployment reintegration activities, practices, and programs.* Centralization of this type of programming across the interagency community has strong

potential to both reduce transaction costs and increase standardization. Both the DoS' FSI and USAID's Staff Care have potential as venues for centralized programming and provision of services, although both would have to be resourced adequately from pooled funds across the interagency community to do so. Moreover, because federal civilians typically do not deploy in units, aggregating individual deployees across agencies into groups and sending them through post-deployment reintegration programs together—and, in doing so, mimicking the unit construct—could be beneficial in multiple ways.

5. *U.S. federal agencies should consider pilot tests of select military reintegration solutions, adapted for their deployed civilian populations.* Promising military post-deployment reintegration practices relevant to the federal civilian population exist and might be beneficial to both DoD and non-DoD federal agencies after they have been adapted for individual organizational needs. The characteristics and needs of a particular agency and civilian population in question will need to be considered carefully to find alignment with a potentially comparable military practice.
6. *Individual agencies and both the DoD and non-DoD federal agency communities should conduct further evidence-based research on civilian deployees and post-deployment reintegration activities.* Systematic evaluation of federal civilian deployment experiences, particularly during the post-deployment stage, is lacking; there has also been no substantial examination into the various categories of personnel eligible for particular activities. More research is needed to explore distinctions between civilian and military deployees, and among different populations of civilian deployees themselves. Furthermore, future research could evaluate in a useful way which activities, practices, and programs facilitate civilian reintegration—the resumption of age, gender, and culturally appropriate roles in the family, community, and workplace, and the process of transitioning back into personal and organizational roles following deployment—most effectively. This research should measure both the effectiveness of the respective activities and programs and the associated cost.

Additional potential areas for future in-depth research on this topic include evidence-based selection of military reintegration programs for adaptation to the civilian population, and efforts to pilot and evaluate new civilian reintegration programs. Finally, future research to explore agencies' incentives for providing civilian reintegration programs, particularly related to incentives to maintain an adequate, satisfied labor pool willing to undertake multiple civilian deployments, might be useful in addressing the benefit to the agencies of providing such services.

Conclusion

Overall, we found little evidence to show that the U.S. federal civilian agencies examined in this report have been systematically thinking about post-deployment reintegration. Although some agencies have devoted resources to the issue, most agencies have little in the way of either (1) an overarching philosophy or conceptualization of post-deployment reintegration, (2) established policy regarding reintegration, or (3) reintegration programs in place for their returning deployees. Significant knowledge and capability gaps exist both within and across the various agencies.

Additionally, there has been little research into civilian post-deployment reintegration activities that might be applicable to and effective within the context of U.S. federal agencies. Although this report explores potential avenues for modeling federal civilian reintegration programs on existing military reintegration programs, the topic poses fruitful ground for further in-depth study on alignment of particular programs with specific civilian populations.

Acknowledgments

We gratefully acknowledge the assistance of several individuals across the U.S. DoD and non-DoD federal agency communities who took the time to speak with us for the purposes of this study—without their participation, this research would not have been possible. At the RAND Corporation, we also thank Susan Marquis, Howard Shatz, and the RAND Initiated Research program for funding this report; Jennifer Lamping Lewis for careful and insightful peer review of the report; John Winkler, Lisa Harrington, and Craig Bond for their management support over the course of the study; Carrie Farmer for providing subject-matter expertise and substantive insights throughout the development of the research; and Barbara Bicksler for communications and editorial support.

Abbreviations

AFI	Air Force Instruction
CBP	U.S. Customs and Border Protection
COSC	Combat Operational Stress Control
DEA	U.S. Drug Enforcement Administration
DHS	U.S. Department of Homeland Security
DoC	U.S. Department of Commerce
DoD	U.S. Department of Defense
DoDD	Department of Defense Directive
DoDI	Department of Defense Instruction
DoS	U.S. Department of State
DSMP	Deployment Stress Management Program
DTC	Deployment Transition Center
EAP	employee assistance program
FAMS	Federal Air Marshal Service
FECA	Federal Employee Compensation Act
FEMA	Federal Emergency Management Agency
FOH	Federal Occupational Health
FSI	Foreign Service Institute
FY	fiscal year
ICE	U.S. Immigration and Customs Enforcement

IRS	Internal Revenue Service
OFDA	Office of Foreign Disaster Assistance
OIE	Office of International Engagement
OPM	Office of Personnel Management
OSCAR	Operational Stress Control and Readiness
PCCC	Post-Combat Case Coordinator
PERSTEMPO	Personnel Tempo
PRT	Provincial Reconstruction Team
PSC	personal services contractor
PTSD	posttraumatic stress disorder
QDDR	*Quadrennial Diplomacy and Development Review*
R3	return, reunion, and reintegration
SIGAR	Special Inspector General for Afghanistan Reconstruction
SSTR	stability, security, transition and reconstruction
TLD	third-location decompression
TSA	Transportation Security Administration
USAID	U.S. Agency for International Development
USCIS	U.S. Citizenship and Immigration Services
USDA	U.S. Department of Agriculture
YRRP	Yellow Ribbon Reintegration Program

CHAPTER ONE

Introduction

Background

Over the past two decades, the United States has deployed an unprecedented number of U.S. federal government civilians to the conflicts in Iraq and Afghanistan to perform a wide variety of tasks—from administrative support to development advice and assistance and diplomatic functions. The use of U.S. federal civilians in overseas contingency operations underwent significant changes during Operation Iraqi Freedom and Operation Enduring Freedom in Afghanistan, particularly during President George W. Bush's second term in office.

During President Bush's first term, U.S. federal civilians from various agencies, including the U.S. Department of State (DoS) and the U.S. Agency for International Development (USAID),[1] deployed in relatively small numbers to work for U.S. Department of Defense (DoD) organizations in Iraq, such as the Office for Reconstruction and Humanitarian Assistance and the Coalition Provisional Authority, or within Provincial Reconstruction Teams (PRTs) that had been established in Afghanistan in November 2002.[2]

---

1 Other participating agencies included, but were not limited to, the U.S. Department of Agriculture (USDA), the U.S. Department of Justice, the U.S. Department of Health and Human Services, the U.S. Department of Commerce (DoC), and the U.S. Department of the Treasury. See Robert M. Perito, *The U.S. Experience with Provincial Reconstruction Teams in Afghanistan: Lessons Identified*, Special Report 152, Washington, D.C.: United States Institute of Peace, October 2005.

2 Note that only three U.S. government agencies were identified as having civilian positions in U.S. military–led PRTs in Afghanistan at this time: DoS, USAID, and USDA. See Perito, 2005.

Although the exact numbers of civilians deployed from 2001 through 2005 are unpublished, the available data indicate that approximately 20 to 40 interagency civilians were deployed throughout this timeframe to the U.S. Central Command area of operation to assist with PRT operations. For example, 13 DoS foreign service officers were serving in PRTs in mid-2005, although the USDA reportedly provided ten PRT advisers in six-month rotations.[3] Interestingly, few civilians were deployed by DoD to these conflicts during this time period.[4]

In President Bush's second term, it became apparent that the U.S. military was not going to make a quick exit from either theater because of rapidly deteriorating security conditions. This point was further emphasized through the publication of DoD Directive (DoDD) 3000.05, which stated that stability operations were "a core U.S. military mission that the Department of Defense shall be prepared to conduct."[5] At approximately the same time, President Bush issued National Security Presidential Directive 44,[6] which charged the Secretary of State with leading integrated U.S. government reconstruction and stabilization efforts; DoS stood up the Office of the Coordinator for Reconstruction and Stabilization to enhance civilian capacity for crises involving complex emergencies; and PRTs were stood up in Iraq to combine "economic, military, and political people in teams to help local and provincial governments."[7] PRTs—modeled after the

---

[3] Perito, 2005.

[4] Molly Dunigan, Susan S. Sohler Everingham, Todd Nichols, Michael Schwille, and Susanne Sondergaard, *Expeditionary Civilians: Creating a Viable Practice of Department of Defense Civilian Deployment*, Santa Monica, Calif.: RAND Corporation, RR-975-OSD, 2016.

[5] DoD Directive 3000.05, *Military Support for Stability, Security, Transition, and Reconstruction (SSTR) Operations*, Washington, D.C.: U.S. Department of Defense, November 28, 2005, p. 2. This directive was updated and formalized into a DoD Instruction in 2009.

[6] National Security Presidential Directive NSPD-44, Management of Interagency Efforts Concerning Reconstruction and Stabilization, Washington, D.C.: White House, December 7, 2005.

[7] Condoleezza Rice as quoted in Cameron S. Sellers, *Provincial Reconstruction Teams: Improving Effectiveness*, dissertation, Naval Postgraduate School, Monterey, Calif., September 2007, p. 17.

Vietnam-era Civil Operations and Revolutionary Development Support program—offered a promising step toward sustained interagency cooperation.[8] By the end of 2006, there were seven U.S. PRTs in Iraq. In January 2007, Bush announced the creation of an additional ten PRTs as part of his "New Way Forward," otherwise known as the "surge."[9] Moreover, unlike the military-led PRTs in Afghanistan, PRTs in Iraq were to be led by the DoS and staffed with civilians to a greater extent.[10]

Meanwhile, numerous non-DoD federal agencies deploy civilian personnel to high-threat environments and high levels of stress that are not active theaters of war. For example, the Office of Foreign Disaster Assistance (OFDA) within USAID regularly deploys Disaster Assistance Response Teams (DARTs) to respond to natural disasters and humanitarian crises. The U.S. State Department has a sizable cadre of foreign service officers and personnel hired through foreign service limited appointments who regularly deploy for lengthy periods of time to perform diplomatic functions. The Drug Enforcement Administration (DEA) has a pool of roughly 700 civilian agents who regularly deploy to high-threat environments, and the Forest Service employs 12,259 personnel in Wildfire Management and has a team of between 20 and 40 personnel who support and deploy with USAID's OFDA. In short, the U.S. federal government deploys civilians to perform a variety of functions, including but not limited to the following:

- disaster relief specialist
- embassy attaché
- diplomatic representative
- economic diplomacy expert
- investment and reconstruction adviser

8 U.S. Joint Forces Command Joint Warfighting Center, "Provincial Reconstruction Teams," pre-doctrinal research white paper No. 07-01, November 21, 2007, p. 16.

9 U.S. Government Accountability Office, *Provincial Reconstruction Teams in Afghanistan and Iraq*, Washington, D.C., GAO-09-86R, October 1, 2008, p. 5.

10 Robert M. Perito, *Provincial Reconstruction Teams in Iraq*, USIP Special Report 185, Washington, D.C.: U.S. Institute of Peace, March 2007.

- project manager
- criminal activity monitor
- counter-drug officer
- international development specialist
- law enforcement adviser
- auditor or investigator
- liaison officer to international missions or organizations
- mentor.

Prior RAND Corporation research[11] focusing on the identification, sourcing, and readiness preparation of U.S. federal civilians for deployment recognized a post-deployment "decompression,"[12] or "redeployment," stage associated with the deployment of civilians from the U.S. interagency community. Considered in its most comprehensive sense, this stage constitutes a variety of efforts to reintegrate deployees (and, ideally, their families) into civilian life following a deployment.[13] Yet, until now, a descriptive account of the specific policies, processes, tools, and outputs associated with this post-deployment reintegration stage of civilian deployment has been lacking, because this stage of civilian deployment has not yet been assessed across organizations of interest. Markedly absent from the literature on post-deployment pro-

---

[11] Molly Dunigan, Michael Schwille, Susanne Sondergaard, Susan S. Sohler Everingham, and Todd Nichols, *Expeditionary Civilians: Creating a Viable Practice of Civilian Deployment Within the U.S. Interagency Community and Among Foreign Defense Organizations*, Santa Monica, Calif.: RAND Corporation, RR-1249-OSD, 2016; Dunigan, Everingham, et al., 2016.

[12] Dunigan, Everingham, et al. (2016) used the term *decompression* to describe the entire post-deployment reintegration process. During the course of this research, we refined the term to be only one of various specific programs. For the remainder of this report, the term decompression will be used in this context and will not be used to represent the entire post-deployment reintegration process.

[13] Reintegration consists of activities, programs, and practices designed to provide support to service members and civilians upon return from a deployment. We define *reintegration* as the resumption of age, gender, and culturally appropriate roles in the family, community, and workplace, and the process of transitioning back into personal and organizational roles following deployment. See the glossary in Appendix A for a full description of post-deployment reintegration.

grams and activities, therefore, is a substantive discussion or evaluation of redeployment practices for these federal civilian deployees, many of whom are in areas where they have a similar likelihood of exposure to combat and related stressors to what is experienced by deployed U.S. troops.

There are some exceptions. In 2010, the DoS' Office of Inspector General[14] and the Broadcasting Board of Governors published a review of support for employees serving in high-stress, high-threat environments.[15] The report recognized the work and progress that the DoS was making in its effort to support employees who were serving in high stress, high threat, unaccompanied posts.[16] The report made several recommendations across topic areas such as mental health support, whether employees took advantage of programs offered to assist them, leadership and stress, options for counseling, administrative hurdles, and family support. The DoS made several improvements based on this report, but many of the recommendations remain pertinent today.[17]

The 2015 DoS and USAID *Quadrennial Diplomacy and Development Review* (QDDR) similarly highlights the importance of the issue of support to returning civilian deployees. In a chapter entitled "Taking Care Of Our People," the document notes the increasing numbers of foreign service officers, civil servants, local staff, and contractors who had worked in challenging locations. It states that:

> The Department and USAID are committed to ensuring that anyone who serves at a dangerous post receives high-quality support prior to, during, and on return from assignment.[18]

---

[14] DoS, Office of the Inspector General, homepage, undated.

[15] DoS, Broadcasting Board of Governors, Office of Inspector General, *Report of Inspection: Review of Support for Employees Who Are Serving or Have Served in High Stress, High Threat, Unaccompanied Posts*, Washington, D.C., Report No. ISP-I-10-44, July 2010.

[16] DoS, Broadcasting Board of Governors, Office of Inspector General, 2010, p. 1.

[17] DoS, Broadcasting Board of Governors, Office of Inspector General, 2010, pp. 11, 12, 23, and 31.

[18] DoS and USAID, *Enduring Leadership in a Dynamic World: Quadrennial Diplomacy and Development Review*, Washington, D.C., 2015, pp. 77–78.

To achieve this, the document states:

> We will expand and update our training and leadership courses to promote resilience in our people. We will increase the capacity of the Office of Medical Services, which will pilot a mentorship program that pairs returnees with staff with high-threat, high-risk (HTHR) experience, and we will expand peer support groups. Lastly, we will examine our policy on Priority Staffing Posts (PSPs) to reflect the challenging and important nature of work in HTHR posts and elsewhere.[19]

In 2015, following the QDDR, USAID released an assessment report, "Stress and Resilience Issues Affecting USAID Personnel in High Operational Stress Environments," which was produced independently by Greenleaf Integrative Strategies. Because the report was produced independently, the views in it did not necessarily reflect the views of USAID or the U.S. government. The report concluded that:

> The USAID workforce is currently exposed to severe and unsustainable levels of stress that (a) are adversely impacting the health of the workforce, (b) very likely are reducing the mission effectiveness of the Agency, and (c) require a coordinated, holistic institutional response.[20]

The research team concluded that the primary sources of stress identified by USAID personnel were related to institutional factors such as excessive workload, leadership deficits, inadequate human resources management and personnel support practices, and poor and unsupportive assignment and fielding practices rather than external contextual factors.[21]

---

19 DoS and USAID, 2015, pp. 77–78.

20 Greenleaf Integrative Strategies, *Assessment of Stress and Resilience Issues Affecting USAID Personnel in High Operational Stress Environments*, Washington, D.C.: United States Agency for International Development, September 2015, p. 1.

21 Greenleaf Integrative Strategies, 2015, p. 6.

Research is clear that combat exposure in service members leads to poorer adjustment[22] once a deployment concludes, as evidenced by a host of consequences including physical health, family and housing problems, employment and financial instability, poor social functioning, suicidality, aggression, violence, and criminality.[23] Successful post-deployment reintegration benefits individual, families, employers, and communities. Although the literature on the post-deployment reintegration *needs* of this population is admittedly incomplete as well, several studies of civilians (both government-employed and contractors) deployed to theaters of conflict over the past two decades do indicate that combat exposure and related stressors correlate with significant levels of deployment-related health conditions for this population.[24] Moreover, media reports provide anecdotal evidence confirming that deployed civilians face similar deployment-related challenges to those experienced by military personnel, both in terms of health conditions and family challenges associated with lengthy deployments.[25] There is a need for more extensive, systematic research on the post-deployment needs of deployed U.S. government civilian personnel; however, such an examination is not the intent of the study at hand.[26] Based on the

---

22 Sarah O. Meadows, Terri Tanielian, and Benjamin Karney, eds., *The Deployment Life Study: Longitudinal Analysis of Military Families Across the Deployment Cycle*, Santa Monica, Calif.: RAND Corporation, RR-1388-A/OSD, 2016.

23 Rajeev Ramchand, Rena Rudavsky, Sean Grant, Terri Tanielian, and Lisa Jaycox, "Prevalence of, Risk Factors for, and Consequences of Posttraumatic Stress Disorder and Other Mental Health Problems in Military Populations Deployed to Iraq and Afghanistan," *Current Psychiatry Reports*, Vol. 17, No. 37, May 2015.

24 Molly Dunigan, Carrie M. Farmer, Rachel M. Burns, Alison Hawks, and Claude Messan Setodji, *Out of the Shadows: The Health and Well-Being of Private Contractors Working in Conflict Environments*, Santa Monica, Calif.: RAND Corporation, RR-420-RC, 2013, pp. 14–16; Greenleaf Integrative Strategies, 2015, p. 1.

25 Robin Wright, "Stress Taking Toll on Foreign Service," *Washington Post*, June 20, 2007; Josh Rogin, "Report: 'Stigma' at State Department for Those Seeking Mental Health Treatment," *Washington Post*, August 5, 2010; Kirk Johnson, "After the Fall," *Washington Post*, January 28, 2007; Jeremiah Goulka, "It Doesn't Take Much to Get PTSD," *Mother Jones*, April 16, 2013.

26 U.S. House of Representatives, Committee on Armed Services, Subcommittee on Oversight and Investigations, *Deploying Federal Civilians to the Battlefield: Incentives, Benefits,*

aforementioned research on the impact of combat exposure on deployed civilians and contractors, here we take as given that the potential for combat exposure, exposure to related stressors, and the long length of civilian deployments to conflict and other high-threat areas indicate a need for civilian post-deployment reintegration support in the general spheres of health and family, at the very least.

Yet, researchers in neither the governmental nor non-governmental spheres to date have catalogued and assessed post-deployment civilian reintegration activities across the breadth of the federal agency community, notwithstanding the tangential relevance of the few individual agency reports mentioned previously. This report therefore endeavors to take an important step toward exploring the specifics of the immediate post-deployment practices of a broad array of U.S. federal agencies with regard to their civilian deployees. To do so, this study seeks to answer three related research questions:

1. What are the current post-deployment reintegration practices for U.S. federal civilian deployees?
2. How do civilian post-deployment reintegration activities, programs, and goals vary across non-DoD federal organizations and in relation to the U.S. DoD?
3. What promising practices can be identified to ensure that civilians receive the support they need to reintegrate into civilian life after deployment?

What Is Post-Deployment Reintegration?

In its March 2017 special issue on military and veteran reintegration, the *American Journal of Orthopsychiatry* made it clear that reintegration

---

and Medical Care, Washington, D.C., April 2008. See also Beth Payne, "Recovering: When Surviving Isn't Enough," *Foreign Service Journal*, January 2008, p. 36; Harry K. Thomas, "Civilians on the Battlefield: Incentives, Benefits and Medical Care for Federal Civilian Employees Deployed to Iraq and Afghanistan," testimony before the House Armed Services Subcommittee on Oversight and Investigations, October 16, 2007, pp. 5–7.

is complex, occurs over time, within an ecological system, and differs by transition circumstances. That special issue included a systematic review of literature, measures of reintegration, and survey results of service member and veteran self-reported needs by Elnitsky, Fisher, and Blevins.[27] Their review led them to define reintegration of military service members and veterans as "both a process and an outcome of resuming roles in family, community, and workplace which may be influenced at different levels of an ecological system."[28] Reintegration can refer to various transitions (e.g., individuals transitioning from post-deployment to home station, from active duty to reserve status, from military to civilian status as a parent, a student, or an employee). Whatever the transition, reintegration is a fluid process that changes over time. Also, reintegration programs may address needs associated with one or all aspects of those transitions.

Elnitsky et al. (2017) identified key reintegration dimensions within an ecological model that capture individual, interpersonal, community organizations, and societal factors. The articles reviewed by Elnitsky and colleagues were categorized by topical focus in order of the most to least articles on the topics included in their review: psychological, family, physical, employment, housing, financial, and education, legal, and spiritual dimensions (see Table 1.1 for examples of programs that address each of these topic areas). Elnitsky and colleagues observed an increase in research on reintegration between 1995 and 2015 and speculated that reduced use of the terms "readjustment" and "transition" beginning around 2009 may be due to the term "reintegration" gaining traction. Elnitsky et al.'s review (2017, p. 118) found that the terms "reintegration" and "community integration" were largely redundant and referred to "participation in life roles;" whereas "readjustment" tended to emphasize psychological functioning; and "transition" tended to emphasize "movement across institutional settings."

---

[27] Christine A. Elnitsky, Michael P. Fisher, and Cara L. Blevins, "Military Service Member and Veteran Reintegration: A Conceptual Analysis, Unified Definition, and Key Domains," *Frontiers in Psychology*, Vol. 8, No. 369, March 14, 2017, pp. 114–128.

[28] Elnitsky, Fisher, and Blevins, 2017, p. 115.

Scope of this Research

The focus of this research was on post-deployment reintegration practices for federal civilians, both those working for DoD and those employed by non-DoD federal agencies.

We designed the study to focus specifically on *post*-deployment practices. Although we recognize that particular pre-deployment and general transition support practices may work in tandem with post-deployment reintegration and may thus be relevant here more broadly, they are outside the scope of this study.[29] Similarly, we did not review programs focusing on transition to secondary education, caregiving, and new employment, although there may be relevant practices in these spheres that could benefit DoD and non-DoD civilian deployers.

To start, the research team selected a simple three-phase deployment cycle to characterize the phase in which a reintegration activity fell, and whether it was therefore in-scope or out-of-scope for this study. The three phases of the cycle are pre-deployment, deployment, and post-deployment (see Figure 1.1). Only activities aligning to the post-deployment phase are included in this study. It should be specifically noted that resilience training was not included in the scope of this research, because it is primarily considered a pre-deployment activity.[30]

The scope of this research is limited in several respects. First, the research focuses specifically on U.S. DoD and non-DoD civilian deployment, though it does consider U.S. military reintegration practice as a comparative case through which to derive lessons regarding potentially promising practices for civilian deployment. We specifically opted to use DoD's military post-deployment reintegration practices as a source of lessons and best practices because of the relative abundance

---

[29] Todd Yosick, Mark Bates, Monique Moore, Chris Crowe, Jennifer Phillips, and John Davison, *A Review of Post-Deployment Reintegration: Evidence, Challenges, and Strategies for Program Development*, Arlington, Va.: Defense Centers of Excellence for Psychological Health and Traumatic Brain Injury, February 2012, p. 3.

[30] Several pre- and post-deployment resilience training programs exist across the services, including Comprehensive Soldier Fitness, Battlemind, Soldier 360, the Marine Combat Operational Stress Control Program, and the DoD-wide Families OverComing Under Stress program. Chapter Two discusses these programs in greater detail.

Figure 1.1
Deployment Cycle

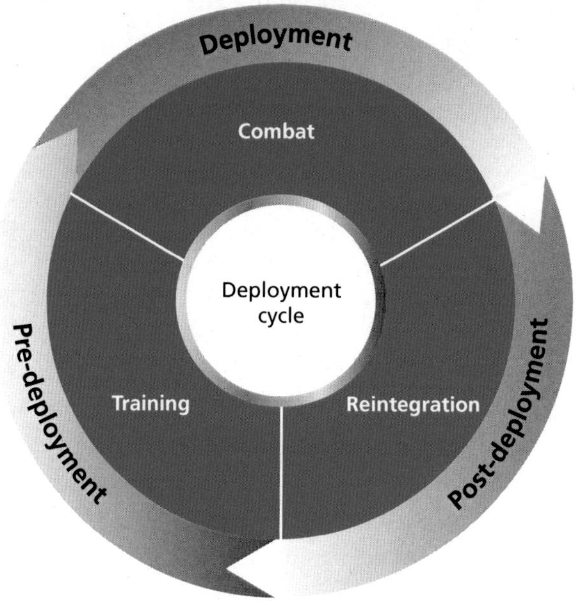

SOURCE: Yosick et al., 2012.

of such programs and the amount of related research on the effectiveness of such programs in meeting service member reintegration needs. Indeed, several studies already identify promising reintegration practices for U.S. service members.

Similarly, we exclude reintegration programs and policies governing veteran support. A large web of services exists and many organizations serve to facilitate veterans' transition to civilian life. For example, faith based organizations are community resources for veterans. A RAND study found that faith-based organizations do more than address the spiritual needs of veterans, but also can address other health and wellness needs.[31] Furthermore, these organizations might

---

31 Laura Werber, Kathryn Pitkin Derose, Mollie Rudnick, Margaret C. Harrell, and Diana Naranjo, *Faith-Based Organizations and Veteran Reintegration: Enriching the Web of Support*, Santa Monica, Calif.: RAND Corporation, RR-931-RC, 2015.

offer a sense of privacy or confidentiality which they may not expect from DoD or U.S. Department of Veterans Affairs programs. Future research to identify reintegration support for civilian deployers should consider drawing from the experiences of the Department of Veterans Affairs.

In contrast, relatively few DoD civilian reintegration policies and practices exist at present. Therefore, although one might surmise the DoD civilian population to better resemble non-DoD civilians in terms of deployment experiences and needs, DoD civilians similarly represent a population on which more extensive research is needed to inform an understanding of their specific reintegration needs and the creation of more-extensive policies and practices to support their post-deployment reintegration. Therefore, we include DoD civilians alongside non-DoD civilians in the study as a population of interest.

Second, the number and range of interviews were not sufficient to provide a complete picture of the causes and effects of any weaknesses in current post-deployment reintegration, and information gathered from interviews should be considered only as an illustrative first attempt at demonstrating the scope and scale of relevant issues associated with such practices, program, and activities.

Approach

The research methodology combined a limited literature review and stakeholder interviews.

The literature review used open-source publications from both academic and government sources, including, for example, refereed psychological health journals, DoD and service-specific policy documents,[32] and independent studies on military and civilian post-

[32] The Office of the Secretary of Defense is the principal staff element of the Secretary of Defense in the exercise of policy development. The Executive Services Division within the Office of the Secretary of Defense "manages the Department of Defense directives and issuances process," which are the overarching policy documents for the Department of Defense. Throughout this report, when *DoD policy* is referenced, we are specifically referencing these policies maintained by the Office of the Secretary of Defense. The military services are the

deployment reintegration activities. We reviewed the websites of the agencies of interest for relevant policies and related documents, as well as government sites (such as the Defense Technical Information Center). We initiated searches for academic sources utilizing the Google Scholar search engine. In addition, we conducted an internal search of RAND and other federally funded research and development center reports, spoke with internal experts at RAND who pointed us toward relevant sources, and received documents from interviewees.

The literature review was not comprehensive, although it covered various policies and practices and relied on prior comprehensive efforts to evaluate reintegration programs. The literature review was designed to assist the study team in understanding the variety of existing DoD, service-specific, and civilian post-deployment reintegration activities, practices, and programs. The research team developed a working definition of *post-deployment integration* based on academic literature and considered DoD and service-specific practices as a baseline from which to compare and potentially draw lessons learned to inform civilian post-deployment reintegration efforts. DoD programs designed specifically for members of the National Guard and U.S. military reserve component were not included in the literature review, although many policies and programs described in Chapter Two have been adapted and adopted by the National Guard and Reserves. The literature reviewed highlighted the priorities, practices, and programs implemented by both DoD and U.S. federal civilian agencies.

The study team then used this research base to prepare for and conduct stakeholder interviews with non-DoD federal agencies.[33] The

---

Air Force, Army, Navy and Marine Corps; for the remainder of this report, the term *services* will be used to refer to these four organizations. Each service enacts specific policy to govern and control their respective organization.

[33] These interviews are attributed anonymously throughout the document in compliance with the U.S. Federal Policy for the Protection of Human Subjects (also known as the Common Rule). Organizational affiliation is included in citations to give a sense of the interviewee's background and experience, but we should note that interviewees were not asked to represent their organizations in a confidential way. Although they were asked to respond based on their professional experiences, they were, in all cases, speaking for themselves rather than for their organizations in an official capacity.

interview sample included 17 offices within seven distinct non-DoD federal agencies, nine interviews across DoD and the military services, and one foreign office (see Table 1.1). The sample ranged across deployees, direct line managers of people deployed, human resources personnel, medical support, and individuals in organizational management positions. Of those interviewed, 28 managed deployed federal civilians and eight had deployed. The research team selected deployees for interviews based on the extent of their first-hand practical experience of reintegrating into civilian life and agency processes following a deployment. The intent of management interviews was to understand post-deployment policies, procedures, and organizational practices affecting civilian deployees. Personnel selected for interviews ranged across employment categories including foreign service professionals, civil service professionals, personal services contractors (PSCs), or a combination of those categories over their career. Although the research team sought to engage a wide range of agencies that deployed people overseas, the interview sample also included two agencies that deploy civilians domestically to high-stress environments (i.e., the Federal Emergency Management Agency [FEMA] and the U.S. Forest Service) in an effort to learn from and inform their post-deployment reintegration practices. We also interviewed one representative from a foreign government office deploying civilians. Of note, we do not include the Intelligence Community within our analysis of civilian post-deployment decompression. The nature of the intelligence mission set and deployed activities are unique among the deployed civilian population such that they may have different reintegration needs. Although the intelligence community is outside the scope of this study, it constitutes a population worthy of future research. The interview protocol is included in Appendix B.

The number and range of interviews were not sufficient to provide a comprehensive picture of the causes and effects of any weaknesses in current post-deployment reintegration practices applicable to the U.S. federal civilian deployee population. However, the information and data gathered from the interviews provided valuable insights regarding the scope and scale of relevant issues associated with such

Table 1.1
Organizations Interviewed

	Number of Personnel Interviewed		
Agency	**Deployees**	**Management**	**Offices Interviewed**
U.S. Agency for International Development	1	3	• U.S. Agency for International Development Staff Care • Office of Foreign Disaster Assistance
U.S. Department of Agriculture		1	• U.S. Forest Service
U.S. Department of Commerce	2		• International Trade Administration • Iraq and Afghanistan Investment and Reconstruction Task Force
U.S. Department of Homeland Security (DHS)	1	7	• U.S. Customs and Border Protection (CBP) • Federal Emergency Management Agency • Office of International Engagement (OIE) • U.S. Citizenship and Immigration Service (USCIS) • U.S. Immigration and Customs Enforcement (ICE) • Transportation Security Administration (TSA)—Federal Air Marshal Service (FAMS)
U.S. Department of Justice		2	• Drug Enforcement Agency
U.S. Department of State	1	5	• Afghanistan and Pakistan Strategic Partnership Office • Bureau of Medical Services • Foreign Service Institute (FSI) • Office of the Director General
U.S. Department of Treasury	1	1	• Office of International Affairs

Table 1.1—Continued

Agency	Number of Personnel Interviewed		Offices Interviewed
	Deployees	Management	
U.S. Department of Defense	2	8	• Department of the Navy—Expeditionary Civilian Program • Department of the Air Force—Expeditionary Civilian Program • DoD Expeditionary Civilian Office • Special Inspector General for Afghanistan Reconstruction (SIGAR)
European Union External Action Office		1	• European Union External Action Service
Total personnel interviewed	8 (22%)	28 (78%)	

practices, highlighting several consistent themes and issues that applied consistently across the agencies in question.

Through the literature review and interviews, we identified a typology of ten reintegration practice areas on which the remainder of the report is focused. These ten reintegration practice areas are depicted in Table 1.2 with examples for each (they are defined in further detail in Chapter Two).

Organization of this Report

The remainder of this report is organized as follows: Chapter Two is an exploration of current DoD and service-specific policy and practice with regard to post-deployment reintegration of U.S. service members. This examination of DoD and service-specific policy and practices for military reintegration serves as a baseline with which to compare U.S. federal agency civilian post-deployment reintegration policies and practices, but also as a more-established case from which to derive promising practices that could potentially inform U.S. federal agency policies and practices on this topic. Chapter Three draws on both the

Table 1.2
Categories of Reintegration Activities

Activity	Examples
Administrative outprocessing	Checklists, turning in equipment, update forms, and final paycheck
Health assessments	Post-deployment health assessments and medical checks
Decompression programs	Third location decompression (TLD) rest and psychoeducation
Post-deployment leave	Administrative or regular leave
Incentives and recognition	Diplomate pay (or hazard pay), awards, and "welcome home" events
Workplace reintegration	Policies to protect office space, and efforts to support return to work
Community and family reintegration	Benefits assistance, family reunion activities, and education
Post-trauma practices	Stress management and psychotherapy
Personnel tracking	Monitoring personnel upon return from a deployment
Individual mobilization augmentee assistance	Assigned case manager, educational websites on reintegration support programs

NOTE: These categories of reintegration activity were compiled from RAND analysis of post-deployment activities used by the DoD and from interviews with non-DoD civilian agencies.

literature review and interview findings to describe the nature of civilian deployments across the variety of U.S. federal agencies studied, exploring current post-deployment reintegration policies and practices in place across this population. Chapter Four concludes the study with findings and recommendations aimed at helping the U.S. federal agency community to improve the post-deployment reintegration policies and practices offered to its civilian deployees, and to standardize such policies and practices to the extent practical in an attempt to (1) ensure that federal agency civilians are treated equally in this regard, and (2) realize efficiencies and potential cost-savings where possible.

CHAPTER TWO

DoD Post-Deployment Reintegration Policies and Practices

In this chapter, we address the need for post-deployment reintegration support and describe DoD policies and programs designed to mitigate negative consequences of deployment. We highlight illustrative programs, policies, and practices that may be helpful to non-DoD federal agencies who deploy personnel to combat zones.[1]

Are Post-Deployment Reintegration Programs Needed?

DoD has highly developed policies and processes to address post-deployment reintegration needs. For example, the United States implemented The Servicemen's Readjustment Act of 1944, or the G.I. Bill, to provide for college and vocational education for returning World War II veterans[2] and a year of unemployment compensation and loans for the veterans to purchase homes and businesses.

The Deployment Life Study was a DoD-commissioned longitudinal study of military families before, during, and after deployment, designed to understand adjustment across five domains: marriage, family, psychological and behavioral health, child and teen well-being,

---

[1] For a thorough review of DoD post-deployment reintegration programs and their impact, see Institute of Medicine, *Returning Home from Iraq and Afghanistan: Assessment of Readjustment Needs of Veterans, Service Members, and Their Families*, Washington, D.C.: National Academies Press, 2013; Yosick et al., 2012.

[2] Public Law 346, Chapter 268, "Servicemen's Readjustment Act of 1944," June 22, 1944.

and military integration.[3] According to that study, most service members and families return to their pre-deployment functions following a deployment—although there are notable exceptions. The study showed that combat exposure, psychological trauma, and physical injury were associated with poorer post-deployment functioning. It is in those populations that post-deployment support programming is most indicated. Researchers found that a significant minority of people experience health problems related to deployment, including mental and physical health. Prevalence rates of post-traumatic stress disorder (PTSD) following combat deployment are wide-ranging and depend on such factors as study cohort, setting, measurement tool, and time since deployment;[4] in addition, the survival rates following being wounded in action have increased since the Vietnam War.[5] Those with physical injuries have additional post-deployment reintegration needs, including access to high-quality health care.

Another foundational report was published by the National Academies of Science, which described military, veteran, and family readjustment needs. Those researchers found that many service members and their families cited an array of health, economic, and social challenges following deployment, and post-deployment programs designed to mitigate those challenges were largely untested.[6] They similarly report that there is a lack of evidence to support *prevention* programs' effectiveness and a need for systematic research and performance measures to guide program implementation.

In 2013, RAND researchers assessed the reintegration needs of National Guard and reserve component members and their families following deployment. They found that some families experienced

---

3 Meadows, Tanielian, and Karney, 2016.

4 Ramchand et al., 2015.

5 Matthew S. Goldberg, *Updated Death and Injury Rates of U.S. Military Personnel During the Conflicts in Iraq and Afghanistan*, Washington, D.C.: Congressional Budget Office, Working Paper 2014-08, December 2014; and Nese DeBruyne, *American War and Military Operations Casualties: Lists and Statistics*, Washington, D.C.: Congressional Research Service, September 24, 2019.

6 Institute of Medicine, 2013.

challenges following deployment associated with emotional or mental health, health care, civilian employment, the spouse/partner relationship, financial or legal matters, child well-being, and education. These challenges emerged over time, following an idiosyncratic trajectory. The researchers found that families experiencing positive outcomes were associated with maintaining good communication, deliberately carving out family time, and making use of reintegration-oriented resources.

RAND researchers identified an extensive web of support resources; research participants often reported that beyond services offered by the service member's unit, private organizations, faith-based organizations, and state and local organizations were helpful in providing support.[7] Although the needs of the National Guard and reserve population likely differ from civilians because civilian deployees transition to a new job (from active duty to their original place of employment), it is reasonable to expect that many of these findings would also apply to federal civilians' reintegration needs following deployment. For example, health care, relationships, financial needs, and child well-being are likely areas of concern throughout post-deployment reintegration in any population.

We know of no studies that identify causal links between post-deployment reintegration programs and successful reintegration, although there is evidence that pre-deployment preparation is associated with better post-deployment outcomes. Research gaps remain in understanding both overall program effectiveness and the needs of specific populations as they reintegrate over time. Nevertheless, the existing policies and practices in DoD offer guidance for non-DoD federal agencies who deploy civilians to combat zones and who want to offer post-deployment programs to support their personnel. The remainder of this chapter provides an overview of the most-relevant policies and practices in DoD and the military services.

---

[7] Laura Werber, Agnes Gereben Schaefer, Karen Chan Osilla, Elizabeth Wilke, Anny Wong, Joshua Breslau, and Karin E. Kitchens, *Support for the 21st-Century Reserve Force: Insights to Facilitate Successful Reintegration for Citizen Warriors and Their Families*, Santa Monica, Calif.: RAND Corporation, RR-206-OSD, 2013.

Post-Deployment Reintegration Policies for Uniformed Personnel

Department of Defense

DoD policy addresses all aspects of the military deployment cycle, to include aspects of post-deployment reintegration. Several DoD Instructions (DoDIs), DoDDs, memoranda, and other policy documents and forms govern pre- and post-deployment activities. Although many of the relevant policy and guidance documents address all three phases of the deployment cycle, we limited our focus to the documents that govern post-deployment practices and goals for the purposes of this study. Chapter One's Table 1.1 lists examples of post-deployment reintegration policies based on the reintegration topic area the policies address.

Service-Specific Post-Deployment Reintegration Policies

Each military service has different missions, priorities, and personnel; therefore, each branch has implemented post-deployment reintegration policies to suit specific service needs. Service-specific reintegration policy varies in its level of formality. Some of the services have general policy guidance and rely on subordinate commands to devise processes and procedures to suit organizational needs, while others have specific policies covering different aspects of the post-deployment cycle in detail. Each service has policy implementing the DoD requirements for health assessments,[8] leave,[9] post-deployment awards and recognition,[10] and tracking of personnel.[11]

Army policy, for example, is very detailed regarding the methods through which soldiers can accrue various types of leave, which is an aspect of decompression following deployment.[12] Commanders are encouraged to grant post-deployment leave "upon permanent change of station" and "after prolonged deployments," among other reasons. Leave granted after deployments is often called "block leave," and the Army encourages its service members to use this leave to the maximum extent available.[13]

The Air Force's home station reintegration policy (Air Force Instruction [AFI] 10-403)[14] provides another illustrative example of a post-deployment reintegration practice. This policy makes clear that home station reintegration "is an ongoing process, NOT a homecoming event." The policy provides maximum flexibility to the individual commands to develop activities and policies best suited to their specific

---

8 U.S. Department of the Air Force, *Deployment Health*, Air Force Instruction 48-122, August 18, 2014c; U.S. Department of the Army, *Army Personnel Policy Guidance*, August 2013; U.S. Department of the Army, "Department of the Army Civilian Post-Deployment Health Reassessment Implementation Guidance," Washington, D.C., memorandum, undated; U.S. Department of the Navy, *Deployment Health Assessment Process*, OPNAVINST 6100.3A, November 10, 2014b.

9 U.S. Department of the Air Force, *Absence and Leave*, Air Force Instruction 36-825, July 8, 2015, p. 13; U.S. Department of the Army, 2013, p. 154; U.S. Department of the Navy, *Naval Military Personnel Manual*, Millington, Tenn., NAVPERS 15560D, August 22, 2002.

10 U.S. Department of the Air Force, *Awards and Decoration Program*, Air Force Policy Directive 36-28, April 26, 2016a, p. 2; U.S. Department of the Army, *Military Awards*, Army Regulation 600-8-22, June 25, 2015c, p. 88; U.S. Department of the Navy, *Military Awards Guidance*, NAVPERSCOM Instruction 1650.3D, April 19, 2016, p. 2.

11 U.S. Department of the Army, *Personnel Accounting and Strength Reporting*, Army Regulation 600-8-6, April 1, 2015b; U.S. Department of the Navy, *Navy Personnel Tempo and Operating Tempo Program*, OPNAVINST 300.13D, March 14, 2014a, p. 7.

12 U.S. Department of the Army, *Leaves and Passes*, Army Regulation 600-8-10, August 4, 2011b.

13 U.S. Department of the Army, 2011b, p. 3.

14 U.S. Department of the Air Force, *Deployment Planning And Execution*, AFI 10-403, September 20, 2012.

populations. The policy also specifically highlights the Deployment Transition Center (DTC) as a place where airmen exposed to "significant risk of death" attend TLD, a reintegration practice described in further detail later in this chapter. The same policy also makes note of the Airman and Family Readiness Centers. With respect to post-deployment activities, this center "play[s] an integral role in reintegration monitoring, family coping skills, assisting with potential at-risk families and collaborating with [other] agencies to ensure smooth family reunions."[15] Reintegration practices are further described in the next section, categorized by the topic areas detailed by Elnitsky and colleagues in 2017.[16]

Types of Reintegration Practices

Because reintegration is a multifaceted process, different programming may be needed to facilitate different aspects of it. Here, we discuss the most-visible programs and practices that have been evaluated and describe the relevant findings and limitations of such studies. DoD programs that have been sustained over time may well be those that leadership believes are most important. Using program size and time since inception as a rough proxy for program utility, we consider how these practices may be applied and benefit non-DoD deployers. The following sections are aligned to the activity types identified in Chapter One's Table 1.1.

Administrative Outprocessing from Theater Following a Deployment

Administrative outprocessing upon return from deployment is a way to cover a checklist of requirements and establish a system of record to document post-deployed status. Outprocessing is mandated and may include a variety of tasks, such as returning equipment, documenting

---

15 For details about these centers, see U.S. Department of the Air Force, 2012, p. 195; U.S. Department of the Air Force, *Airman and Family Readiness Centers*, Air Force Instruction 36-3009, July 16, 2014b.

16 Elnitsky, Fisher, and Blevins, 2017, p. 115.

combat exposure, taking a tuberculosis test, drawing serum samples, finalizing any disciplinary actions, and updating health records.[17] U.S. Army Europe, for example, relies on a half-day model for administrative outprocessing. Upon arrival at the home station, the first steps performed are "personnel accountability, sensitive item accountability, [and] sensitive item turn-in." The process varies by command, but many of the administrative tasks are completed early in the reintegration process.[18] In another example, a 2005 post-deployment processing checklist for military personnel includes a list of commanders, Office of Primary Responsibility or Office of Collateral Responsibility, the due date, and the date completed with signature. Tasks include "turn-in weapon and/or ammunition, process return with unit monitor, process travel voucher with Finance [and] request R&R/Compensatory Time and Leave with Squadron Commander/Designee."[19]

Health Assessments

Based on DoDD 5124.02 and Sections 1074a, 10149, and 10206 of Title 10 of the U.S. Code, DoDI 6200.06 establishes annual requirement for a Periodic Health Assessment.[20] To specifically address service members participating in contingency operations as directed by Section 1074(m) of Title 10 of the U.S. Code, DoDI 6490.12 requires pre- and post-deployment health assessments and reassessments for service members and a review by an in-person mental health practitioner either during in-theater medical outprocessing or within 30 days of returning home.[21] These interviews are to be conducted by either an

---

17 U.S. Department of the Army, *Department of the Army Global War on Terrorism (GWOT) Post Conflict/Mobilization Personnel Operations*, Deployment Cycle Support (DCS) Concept Plan (CONPLAN), May 2, 2003a.

18 U.S. Department of the Army, *Personnel Recovery*, Army Regulation 525-28, March 2010a.

19 U.S. Department of the Air Force, *Post Deployment Processing Checklist (Military Personnel)*, August 2005.

20 DoDI 6200.06, *Periodic Health Assessment (PHA) Program*, Washington, D.C.: U.S. Department of Defense, September 8, 2016.

21 DoDI 6490.12, *Mental Health Assessments for Service Members Deployed in Connection with a Contingency Operation*, U.S. Department of Defense, February 26, 2013, p. 5.

independently licensed mental health professional or a trained and certified health care provider (e.g., a physician, physician assistant, nurse practitioner, advanced practice nurse, independent duty corpsman, special forces medical sergeant, independent duty medical technician, or independent health services technician). The pre-deployment DD Form 2795[22] should take place 30 days before departure, and the post-deployment DD Form 2796[23] should be conducted 30 days after the return from deployment. Individuals who indicate health concerns will also be referred for a meeting with a trained health care provider.[24]

Those service members and civilians who complete DD Form 2796 must also complete a post-deployment health reassessment (DD Form 2900) between 90 and 180 days after their return home. Upon completion of the reassessment, a trained health care provider will discuss health concerns and make necessary referrals. The health care providers are also instructed to educate individuals on post-deployment health readjustment issues and provide information on resources available for assistance.[25] Finally, each service has implemented administration of its own DoD-mandated mental health assessments.[26]

Evidence suggests that service members underreport symptoms on these health assessments to avoid referral for health care. In a 2011 study, researchers anonymously surveyed soldiers who were simultaneously undergoing post-deployment health assessments. The anonymous survey revealed significantly higher reports of depression, PTSD, suicidal ideation, and a desire to receive care than were picked up by

---

[22] U.S. Department of Defense, "Pre-Deployment Health Assessment," DD Form 2795, September 2012b.

[23] U.S. Department of Defense, "Post Deployment Health Assessment (PDHA)," DD Form 2796, October 2015a.

[24] DoDI 6490.03, *Deployment Health*, U.S. Department of Defense, June 19, 2019, pp. 28-29.

[25] DoDI 6490.03, 2019, p. 31.

[26] DoD, *Report to the Congressional Defense Committees in Response to Section 702 of the National Defense Authorization Act for Fiscal Year 2012 (Public Law 112-81): Mental Health Assessments for Members of the Armed Forces Deployed in Support of a Contingency Operation*, Washington, D.C., July 2013.

the identifiable post-deployment health assessment screening.[27] Further research to identify ways to increase the reliability and validity of responses might help ensure that those in need of care receive it.

Decompression

The services maintain several distinct decompression programs. *Decompression* is defined as a process designed to help personnel returning from deployment to and to promote a positive psychological response to deployment trauma. The Air Force maintains an exemplar TLD program at the Air Force DTC in Germany at the Ramstein Air Base,[28] which serves as a rest stop between combat deployment and return home. It is designed for service members with extensive combat exposure and serves all military branches, plus National Guard, reserves, and civilians. The program is mandated for service members in specified job fields and mission sets. The DTC is a four-day program consisting of three core elements: rest and recuperation; debriefing surrounding deployment experiences; and preparation for reintegration with friends and family. Between 2010 and 2018, approximately 13,000 individuals attended the program. The DTC mission is "To provide critical reintegration skills and decompression opportunities for redeployers."[29]

The Marine Corps Special Operations Command Performance and Resiliency Program is a multifaceted program that provides post-deployment activities to support redeploying Marine Corps forces. TLD is also a key element of this program. The Marines offer TLD for specialized occupations, such as Explosives Ordnance Disposal and Personnel Retrieval and Processing.

---

27 Christopher H. Warner, George N. Appenzeller, Thomas Grieger, Slava Belenkiy, Jill Brietbach, Jessica R. Parker, Carolynn M. Warner, and Charles W. Hoge, "Importance of Anonymity to Encourage Honest Reporting in Mental Health Screening After Combat Deployment," *Archives of General Psychiatry*, Vol. 68, No. 10, October 2011, p. 1065.

28 Ramstein Air Base, "Air Force Deployment Transition Center," webpage, undated.

29 U.S. Air Force, Deployment Transition Center, "Comprehensive Airman Fitness Brochure," September 2018.

Research to date has not demonstrated the effectiveness of TLD practices.[30] In 2016, Schneider and colleagues reported that DTC participants exhibited "lower levels of distress, depressive and [post-traumatic stress] symptoms, relationship conflict, and emotional problems" compared with the weighted control group.[31] Shortly thereafter, a RAND research team conducted an independent study and found that participation in DTC had ". . . no effect on reducing the number of clinically diagnosable cases of mental health conditions post-deployment, [but] there was some evidence to suggest that it may have improved reintegration outcomes," specifically with regard to alcohol use. The same report explains that although participants surveyed enjoyed TLD, they did not display any improvements in psychological or behavioral health compared with a matched control group. The researchers also used Schneider and colleagues' data and arrived at different conclusions.[32]

Post-Deployment Leave

It is logical to think that rest, recuperation, and a break from work would be helpful in some way to the service member, either at home or in some third location. However, we found no research to support post-deployment leave being necessary for successful reintegration. Although not typically mandated, a week or two of post-deployment leave is customary upon redeployment, subject to the commander's

---

[30] Erik De Soir, "Psychological Adjustment After Military Operations: The Utility of Post-deployment Decompression for Supporting Health Readjustment," in Steven V. Bowles and Paul T. Bartone, eds., *Handbook of Military Psychology: Clinical and Organizational Practice*, Cham, Switzerland: Springer, 2017.

[31] Kristin G. Schneider, Serena Bezdjian, Danielle Burchett, William C. Isler, David Dickey, and Howard N. Garb, "The Impact of the United States Air Force Deployment Transition Center on Postdeployment Mental Health Outcomes," *Military Psychology*, Vol. 28, No. 2, 2016, p. 101.

[32] Terry L. Schell, Coreen Farris, Jeremy N. V. Miles, Jennifer Sloan, and Deborah M. Scharf, *The Air Force Deployment Transition Center: Assessment of Program Structure, Process, and Outcomes*, Santa Monica, Calif.: RAND Corporation, RR-918-OSD, 2016, p. 50; Jennifer L. Marino, *Enhancing Resilience Through Post-Deployment Decompression: A Softer Approach to Sharpening the Warrior Edge*, master's degree research paper, Marine Corps University, 2012.

discretion. Such periods of leave can operate as transitional periods for units in some cases, with certain members of a unit leaving for follow-on assignments and new personnel arriving to fill those vacant positions.[33] AFI 10-403[34] identifies the requirements for redeployment, which it specifies in Section 7.5.8.2, "Civilian and ARC [air reserve component] personnel are not authorized leave en route." Therefore, it may be important to identify or establish policies to allow for post-deployment leave on return from a combat deployment for Air Force personnel. However, research does not show that leave time following a deployment improves health outcomes.[35] It is possible, albeit ethically challenging, to conduct a randomized clinical trial to assess the effect of post-deployment leave on post-deployment reintegration. That would mean withholding that transition time (i.e., break or downtime) from a group of service members returning from combat operations. Perhaps a comparison of the timing of post-deployment leave may be more palatable to institutional review boards charged with human subjects' protection. Similar to the realization that post-deployment health assessments should be conducted 90-180 days following a deployment (using DD Form 2900),[36] postponing leave could be found to be more helpful somehow in post-deployment reintegration.

Incentives and Recognition

We know of no research on whether awards and recognition facilitate post-deployment reintegration, but it is conceivable they offer recipients a sense of pride. A key informant from the interviews described in Chapter Three indicated that the DoD expeditionary civilian workforce is trying to increase public recognition of deployed civilian contri-

---

33 U.S. Department of the Army, 2011b.

34 U.S. Department of the Air Force, 2012.

35 Jamie G. H. Hacker Hughes, N. Mark Earnshaw, Neil Greenberg, Rod Eldridge, Nicola T. Fear, Claire French, Martin P. Deahl, and Simon Wessely, "The Use of Psychological Decompression in Military Operational Environments," *Military Medicine*, Vol. 173, No. 6, June 2008.

36 U.S. Department of Defense, "Post-Deployment Health Re-Assessment (PDHRA)," DD Form 2900, October 2015b.

butions by rewarding deployees with medals and other awards.[37] Under current military practice, almost everyone who serves on a deployment receives some sort of award or recognition.[38] Depending on the location of the deployment and categorization of service, deployees could be eligible for a campaign medal, overseas tour recognition, and/or performance award. Although debate exists over the eligibility and conditions for these awards, campaign awards are typically based on location and performance awards are based on the unit level and the commander's discretion.[39]

Community and Family Reintegration

Community and family reintegration is a component of many other post-deployment reintegration programs and is prioritized in several distinct voluntary programs. One of the most prominent programs is the Yellow Ribbon Program, which was codified in the U.S. Code of Federal Regulations in 2009 to provide educational benefits to eligible service members, veterans and their dependents.[40] The Yellow Ribbon Reintegration Program (YRRP) is a DoD-wide umbrella of programs and events to help National Guard and Reserve service members and their families discover local resources before, during, and after deploy-

---

37 Dunigan, Everingham, et al., 2016.

38 As an example of this, the Navy Command Return, Reunion, and Reintegration (R3) program mandates that command leadership "provide official recognition at events such as All Hands calls, Sailor of the Quarter presentations, Hail and Farewell, and by way of command newsletters, awards, and Sailor/spouse/family letters of appreciation," (see U.S. Department of the Navy, "Command Return, Reunion, and Reintegration (R3) Program Standard Operating Procedure (SOP)," memorandum from Parent Command, August 2011, p. 2).

39 DoDI 1348.33, *DoD Military Awards and Recognition Program*, Washington, D.C.: U.S. Department of Defense, December 21, 2016; Department of Defense Manual 1348.33, *Manual of Military Decorations and Awards: DoD Service Awards—Campaign, Expeditionary, and Service Medals*, Vol. 2, U.S. Department of Defense, December 21, 2016a; Department of Defense Manual 1348.33, *Manual of Military Decorations and Awards: DoD Service Awards: DoD-Wide Personal Performance and Valor Decorations*, Vol. 3, U.S. Department of Defense, December 21, 2016b.

40 Code of Federal Regulations Title 38, Pensions, Bonuses, and Veterans' Relief, Section 21.9700, Chapter 1, Yellow Ribbon G.I. Education Enhancement Program.

ment. Many of the activities available during the post-deployment phase are practical: record-processing, veteran benefits eligibility and enrollment support through the U.S. Department of Veterans Affairs, career counseling, medical benefits and TRICARE counseling, assistance with financial and credit issues, safety briefings from local law enforcement officials, and "welcome home" activities.[41] The YRRP also has activities that address psychological, behavioral, social and family issues; spiritual fitness; and relevant post-deployment events and resources. The program also provides referrals for treatment, family and relationship workshops, and counseling.[42]

Beyond Yellow Ribbon is an extension of the YRRP under which Congress funds a handful of states that are given freedom to design programs to "provide a variety of support resources to service members returning from deployment, including employment counseling, behavioral health counseling, suicide prevention and referrals to other providers, among other services."[43] Many of the state Beyond Yellow Ribbon programs examined by a 2015 RAND study are directed toward employment opportunities. However, some are more comprehensive, such as the New Hampshire Care Coordination Program, which provides support for mental health, homelessness, and suicide prevention, in addition to employment opportunities.[44]

The services and service component commands maintain their own reintegration programs. For example, the U.S. Army European Command has used a reintegration model consisting of half-day sessions in which the soldier is slowly reintroduced to family and home life.[45] The checklist of activities and briefings are completed prior to block leave. Briefings include reunion training, suicide awareness and prevention training, and various briefings on such topics as how to iden-

---

[41] Yosick et al., 2012, p. 56.

[42] Yosick et al., 2012, p. 57.

[43] Laura Werber, Jennie W. Wenger, Agnes Gereben Schaefer, Lindsay Daugherty, and Mollie Rudnick, *An Assessment of Fiscal Year 2013 Beyond Yellow Ribbon Programs*, Santa Monica, Calif.: RAND Corporation, RR-965-OSD, 2015, p. 1.

[44] Werber et al., 2015, p. 51.

[45] U.S. Department of the Army, 2010a.

tify signs and symptoms of distress, post-deployment stress, changes in relationships, and communication.[46] The U.S. Marines Corps uses Marine Operational Stress Training, also known as Deployment Cycle Training, which entails a series of informational briefs focused on family transition, both directly following redeployment and again 60 to 120 days following redeployment.[47]

Post-Trauma Practices

Combat exposure is a significant predictor of PTSD.[48] Significant efforts are underway to prevent the development of PTSD and other posttraumatic reactions, such as depression and substance abuse.[49] Resilience building programs are the most established of these programs, developed with the notion that resilience can prevent psychological health consequences of war. These programs are administered across the deployment cycle (before, during, and after) and have multiple components. Some of these programs are further described below, and non-DoD agencies may consider incorporating aspects of these programs to support their deployers.

Combat Operational Stress Control (COSC) was initially developed by the Navy for marines in 2007.[50] At this point in time, and as delineated in further detail below, each service uses variants of COSC.[51]

The Navy COSC program has mandatory pre-deployment, deployment, and post-deployment phases. The deployment phase

---

46 U.S. Department of the Army, 2010a.

47 Yosick et al., 2012, p. 37.

48 Ramchand et al., 2015, p. 37; Institute of Medicine, *Preventing Psychological Disorders in Service Members and Their Families: An Assessment of Programs*, Washington, D.C.: National Academies Press, 2014.

49 Institute of Medicine, 2014.

50 U.S. Department of the Navy, Office of the Chief Naval Officer, *Combat and Operational Stress Control and Warrior Transition Program Administration*, NAVADMIN 182/07, July 23, 2007.

51 Field Manual 4-02.51, *Combat and Operational Stress Control*, Washington, D.C.: Headquarters, U.S. Department of the Army, July 6, 2006; U.S. Department of the Air Force, *Disaster Mental Health Response & Combat and Operational Stress Control*, Air Force Instruction 44-153, May 29, 2014a.

includes "ongoing prevention, support, and treatment for stress and stress related injuries (if needed)," as well as a three- to five-day decompression period. Post-deployment COSC simply involves the mental health assessments that are required by DoD.[52] As part of COSC, the Warrior Transition Program is an in-theater stop that includes "combat stress mitigation and required decompression time" and "small group discussions facilitated by accredited professional and focused on various topics including . . . combat and operational stress briefings."[53]

The Marine Corps' COSC program is focused in large part on pre-deployment activities, such as building "psychological resilience and the long-term health of Marines, attached Sailors, and their families."[54] However, the Marine Operational Stress Control and Readiness (OSCAR) teams operating as part of COSC focus on activities during and after a deployment. OSCAR teams consist of mentors, medical and religious personnel, and mental health providers. The teams are maintained in each battalion or squadron to "prevent, identify, and reduce stress issues as early as possible."[55] In 2015, RAND researchers evaluated the OSCAR program using a quasi-experimental study design, comparing marines who deployed in battalions that had OSCAR teams and Marines who deployed with battalions that did not. This study found that the OSCAR program had a significant impact on marines' help-seeking behavior and recommending that others seek help. However, the research found no other short- or long-term effects from the OSCAR teams, including effects on the "expectancies of stress response and recovery, perceived support for help-seeking, or health outcomes."[56]

---

[52] U.S. Department of the Navy, 2007.

[53] U.S. Department of the Navy, 2007.

[54] Marine Corps Order 5351.1, *Combat and Operational Stress Control Program*, U.S. Department of the Navy, Headquarters, U.S. Marine Corps, February 22, 2013.

[55] Marine Corps Order 5351.1, 2013, p. 2-1; U.S. Department of the Navy, U.S. Marine Corps, *Operational Stress Control and Readiness Training Guidance*, MARADMIN 59/11, October 2011.

[56] Christine Anne Vaughan, Carrie M. Farmer, Joshua Breslau, and Crystal Burnette, *Evaluation of the Operational Stress Control and Readiness (OSCAR) Program*, Santa Monica, Calif.: RAND Corporation, RR-562-OSD, 2015, pp. 26 and 28.

In addition to the OSCAR teams, other elements of the Marine COSC program are the in-theater and in-garrison decompression periods. Units returning from deployment are offered two decompression periods if possible: a three-to-five day "operational pause" before departing theater, and a five-day period in garrison prior to leave.[57]

The Air Force maintains both disaster mental health teams and COSC teams. The disaster mental health teams provide services to "individuals directly involved in all-hazard incident or combat and operational stress."[58] The Air Force COSC program also has a large component focused on pre-deployment activities.

The Army Field Manual on COSC addresses post-deployment screening, reintegration training, and referrals, and states, "[end-of-tour stress management] is essential to reduce mental problems with Soldiers returning to their home station and/or families" through such activities as recognition, events, and homecoming-reunion debriefings.[59] The Army operates a COSC website that describes several programs and resources to support soldiers and leaders.[60] It explains the signs and symptoms of combat stress and links individual symptoms to resources designed to address them.

Beyond COSC, the Army used the Battlemind program for resilience building, which is now called Resilience Training.[61] One of its components, Battlemind Debriefing, was used at different times during and after combat deployment to deal with the cumulative effects of deployment.[62] In 2009, researchers conducted a randomized clinical trial to study Battlemind's effectiveness. Based on a follow-up survey administered four months after participation in the program, Battlemind Debriefing participants were found to have a lower incidence of

---

[57] U.S. Department of the Navy, U.S. Marine Corps, *Combat Operational Stress Control (COSC) Program*, Marine Corps Bulletin 6490, September 18, 2008, p. 6.

[58] U.S. Department of the Air Force, 2014a, p. 7.

[59] Field Manual 4-02.51, 2006.

[60] Army Public Health Center, "Combat Stress Control," U.S. Department of the Army, webpage, last updated December 15, 2017.

[61] Institute of Medicine, 2014.

[62] Institute of Medicine, 2014, p. 88.

PTSD symptoms, depression symptoms, and sleep problems than were standard stress education program participants. Small group participants reported fewer PTSD symptoms and sleep problems, and large group participants reported lower PTSD symptoms and stigma as well as fewer depression symptoms.[63] This program is now considered part of the resilience building suite of programs, which are mandated with training delivered during the duty day.

Additionally, the Army offers specialized, voluntary programs directed at soldiers experiencing PTSD. For example, the Fort Hood Resilience and Restoration Center's Warrior Combat Stress Resilience Program is a comprehensive treatment program for soldiers with clinical PTSD diagnoses. It consists of a three-week intensive day treatment immersion program followed by ten weeks of individualized care.[64]

Pre-trauma practices delivered before or during a combat deployment are based on sound practices but have also not been shown to be effective at mitigating adverse effects of combat exposure. In 2011, Meredith and colleagues reviewed 270 documents on resilience building programs and found only 11 randomized controlled trials. Those trials produced mixed results, none of which found evidence for reduced impairment post-deployment.[65]

Personnel Tracking Procedures

Before employers can offer reintegration support, they must identify who needs that support. Therefore, one way to reduce barriers to

---

63 Amy B. Adler, Paul D. Bliese, Dennis McGurk, Charles W. Hoge, and Carl Andrew Castro, "Battlemind Debriefing and Battlemind Training as Early Interventions with Soldiers Returning From Iraq: Randomization by Platoon," *Journal of Consulting and Clinical Psychology*, Vol. 77, No. 5, October 2009.

64 Robin M. Weinick, Ellen Burke Beckjord, Carrie M. Farmer, Laurie T. Martin, Emily M. Gillen, Joie D. Acosta, Michael P. Fisher, Jeffrey Garnett, Gabriella C. Gonzalez, Todd C. Helmus, Lisa H. Jaycox, Kerry Reynolds, Nicholas Salcedo, and Deborah M. Scharf, *Programs Addressing Psychological Health and Traumatic Brain Injury Among U.S. Military Servicemembers and Their Families*, Santa Monica, Calif.: RAND Corporation, TR-950-OSD, 2011, p. 51.

65 Lisa S. Meredith, Cathy D. Sherbourne, Sarah J. Gaillot, Lydia Hansell, Hans V. Ritschard, Andrew M. Parker, and Glenda Wrenn, *Promoting Psychological Resilience in the U.S. Military*, Santa Monica, Calif.: RAND Corporation, MG-996-OSD, 2011.

receipt of reintegration services would be to track deployers so they can be informed of programming, reminded of health assessment, and provided general information to assist deployees and their families. A database is necessary for tracking information about an individual's deployment and health and social status. Checklists and required forms linked to tracking systems are used to populate the database. Each military service maintains personnel tracking systems. For example, the Navy's PERSTEMPO (Personnel Tempo) database tracks days deployed and associated pay.[66] Personnel tracking enables an employer to manage pay and benefits and to offer services as needed. Thus, administrative and personnel tracking systems should be considered a precursor to delivery of reintegration support and a prerequisite for organizations deploying employees.

Services for Individual Mobilization Augmentees

DoD published DoDI 1235.11, "Management of Individual Mobilization Augmentees (IMAs)," which addresses the assignment, training, and payment of IMAs (those service members who deploy alone with units other than their own).[67] The Navy maintains a robust website for individual augmentees to highlight preparation and return requirements and available resources. The material on the Navy's R3 website guides individual augmentees through the reintegration process.[68] The site also contains all Navy messages and policies regarding individual augmentees,[69] which may offer important guidance to U.S. federal agencies who rely on a similar civilian deployment model. The Navy also identifies a single support contact, individual augmentee con-

---

[66] DoD, *Privacy Impact Assessment (PIA) for the Personnel Tempo (PERSTEMPO) Department of the Navy, Bureau of Naval Personnel*, DD Form 2930, November 2008.

[67] Department of Defense Instruction 1235.11, *Management of Individual Mobilization Augmentees (IMAs)*, Washington, D.C.: U.S. Department of Defense, July 10, 2015.

[68] U.S. Department of the Navy, U.S. Fleet Forces Command, "Return, Reintegration, & Re-Deployment (R3)," *Navy Individual Augmentee*, webpage, undated-b.

[69] U.S. Department of the Navy, U.S. Fleet Forces Command, "Navy IA Messages and Policy," *Navy Individual Augmentee*, webpage, undated-a.

sultants, to connect combat deployers with needed resources (a "case manager" approach).

DoD Reintegration Program Evaluation

Although there is research to support some of the OSCAR and Battlemind programs described earlier in this chapter, research on the effectiveness of most post-deployment reintegration programs is lacking.[70] It is difficult to conduct rigorous program evaluations to assess effectiveness in part because of the need to randomize service members to "non-program" conditions, which may be seen as withholding needed services from a vulnerable population by human subjects protections boards. Some programs do evaluate themselves, but often to a limited extent, with satisfaction measures that cannot determine program effectiveness. A clear understanding of the effectiveness of existing reintegration programs may be the best guide to developing and implementing effective services for other populations. Unfortunately, the large majority of existing programs are not supported by clear evidence of their utility. This represents another essential area for future research. Mapping the evidence and the quality of the program evaluation research to determine which programs are effective and under what circumstances is needed for selecting programs to draw upon to inform reintegration practices for non-uniformed individuals. To this end, there have already been substantive efforts to document the existence of programs and assess their effectiveness reflect some progress. DoD commissioned RAND researchers to catalog all existing psychological health and traumatic brain injury treatment programs in DoD. RAND created a searchable catalog of 211 programs that describes the purpose and approach to each program.[71] Eleven of those programs

---

[70] Institute of Medicine, 2014.

[71] RAND Corporation, "Catalog of Psychological Health and Traumatic Brain Injury Programs," webpage, undated.

were selected for further evaluation based on programmatic size, reach, and other criteria deemed important by the DoD research sponsor.[72]

Programmatic evaluations are limited by the extent to which program processes and outcomes are measured and how consistently the program is being implemented. Therefore, many program evaluations completed to date are process evaluations that assess program implementation to ensure fidelity to program intentions. To our knowledge, a cataloguing of post-deployment reintegration programs that target conditions other than psychological health and traumatic brain injury has not been completed. That effort could enable better-informed decisions about adopting DoD programs for different cohorts. It is important to note that research on the effectiveness of the programs discussed above remains inconclusive. Reliance on program evaluation is growing and much research is underway to assess the utility of program components, program fidelity, and program outcomes.

Summary

Substantial programmatic efforts to prepare service members for combat deployments and to support them in a way that mitigates post-deployment impairment exist, but research remains inconclusive on the effectiveness of these programs. Psychological preparation, in the form of resilience building, education, and peer support, makes up the largest proportion of programs to support post-deployment reintegration. Establishing evidentiary support is methodologically challenging because of the need to randomize people to control interventions, potentially withholding helpful services, or to identify matched samples on demographics and types of combat exposure and circumstances. Nevertheless, these practices can still offer useful insights for developing post-deployment programs for non-DoD agencies.

There may well be existing programs that can provide reintegration support, in addition to other support throughout the deployment cycle. For example, nonmedical counseling programs such as Military

72 For more information, see RAND Corporation, undated.

OneSource may address any number of post-deployment reintegration issues in service members and their families.[73] Non-DoD agencies may want to look more broadly at existing support programs that could be helpful during the post-deployment reintegration process.

In a 2013 survey of National Guard and reserve component member reintegration needs, respondents who used the services reported them as helpful—specifically, unit-sponsored resources in preparation for a family reunion, the YRRP and faith-based organizations, Military OneSource, other military programs, and civilian resources.[74] Federal agencies might consider drawing on those programs and models of reintegration efforts.

Personnel tracking using a database to record deployment characteristics and administrative requirements, such as equipment review and health assessments, is important to consider. Post-deployment leave, awards, and recognition are practices that are not supported by evidence to date but may be helpful for non-DoD agencies wanting to mirror DoD practices to align post-deployment experiences. Research on the utility of these practices is needed. Some evidence indicates community reintegration and family support practices can be helpful. Although substantial efforts to prevent psychological health impairment following deployment exist, none have demonstrated effectiveness to date. A substantial body of literature exists on clinical practices to reduce PTSD using psychotherapy and medications.[75] Overcoming barriers to PTSD treatment is an important topic for consideration by non-DoD federal agencies deploying civilians, although beyond the scope of the current discussion of post-deployment reintegration.

Specific practices that non-DoD agencies should consider include

---

[73] Thomas E. Trail, Laurie T. Martin, Lane F. Burgette, Linnea Warren May, Ammarah Mahmud, Nupur Nanda, and Anita Chandra, *An Evaluation of U.S. Military Non-Medical Counseling Programs*, Santa Monica, Calif.: RAND Corporation, RR-1861-OSD, 2017.

[74] Werber et al., 2013.

[75] Management of Posttraumatic Stress Disorder Work Group, *VA/DoD Clinical Practice Guideline for the Management of Posttraumatic Stress Disorder and Acute Stress Disorder*, version 3.0, Washington, D.C.: U.S. Department of Veterans Affairs and U.S. Department of Defense, 2017.

- using personnel tracking of deployment characteristics (length, location, combat exposure) and health status.
- requiring a post-deployment health assessment.
- employing a case-management approach to tracking health status and matching available resources to individual needs.
- researching to understand the value and optimal length and timing of a designated period of rest following a combat deployment.
- ensuring that families of combat deployees are aware of and can access an extensive web of existing family and community support resources.

There remains a need to evaluate the components of these programs and their overall effectiveness. In assessing the extent to which components of the above programs might be appropriate for translation to a civilian setting, the specific need for post-deployment reintegration within the organization and its employees should be well understood. Chapter Three describes the existing post-deployment reintegration practices in federal civilian agencies and some descriptions of civilian deployees' stated needs and desires for such policies and programs to support them as they return from a deployment.

CHAPTER THREE

Federal Civilian Post-Deployment Reintegration Practices and Experiences

In this chapter, which is drawn from information obtained from a literature review augmented by interviews as described in Chapter One, we describe key characteristics of the federal agencies that took part in interviews for this research and the types of missions they traditionally support, and details the nature of civilian deployments across these U.S. federal agencies. We then briefly review the limited existing policy relevant to post-deployment reintegration for these civilian deployees. Finally, we turn to an analytic review of existing reintegration practices and related assessments, categorizing each agency by the types of reintegration practices they provide and comparing and contrasting these with the DoD and service-specific practices elaborated in Chapter Two. This comparison allows us to derive applicable lessons for enhancing, strengthening, and systematizing civilian post-deployment reintegration practice across the U.S. federal agency community.

Size and Scope of Federal Civilian Deployment by Organization

The U.S. government deploys civilians overseas to perform a wide variety of functions. Individuals interviewed during this research performed the following roles while deployed:[1]

---

[1] It is worth noting that these individuals might not be representative of the entire range of non-DoD federal civilian deployees; nonetheless, their activities indicate at least a partial list of functions performed by civilian deployees overseas.

- disaster relief specialist
- embassy attaché
- diplomatic representative
- economic diplomacy expert
- investment and reconstruction adviser
- project manager
- criminal activity monitor
- counter-drug officer
- international development specialist
- law enforcement adviser
- auditor or investigator
- liaison officer to international missions or organizations
- mentor.

Deployed U.S. federal civilians work at a variety of locations: some in embassies or deployed missions, some with the military, and others in local communities or as part of international missions. In addition to the various deployed roles, there is significant variation in the numbers of people deployed by different U.S. agencies, including the nature, length, and regularity of their deployments, which we discuss later in this chapter.

Unlike the uniformed military and foreign service officers, overseas deployment is not necessarily a standard part of a career for many government civilian employees. Overseas deployments can either be driven by the short-term needs of the organization, or as a career development posting. For some organizations, conventional overseas deployment can be such a small proportion of their overall activities or so irregular that they do not have a foreign service cadre. The conflicts in Iraq and Afghanistan over the past decade have driven the demand for increased deployment of civilian personnel in support of U.S. government efforts, leading to increased numbers of civil servants deploying.

The three main employment categories discussed in this study are civil service, foreign service, and PSCs. *Civil service employees* are defined in U.S. law as "all appointive positions in the executive, judicial, and legislative branches of the Government of the United States, except positions in the uniformed services."[2] When an agency has both a civil service and foreign service cadre, *civil service* refers to staff whose principal duties and employment are within the United States.[3] *Foreign service* refers to those who are employed within the foreign service career cadre of the department or agency, including both foreign service officers and foreign service specialists.[4] A PSC is characterized by "the employer-employee relationship it creates between the Government and the contractor's personnel."[5] For the purposes of this study, it refers to all employees hired under a Title 48 PSC arrangement.

U.S. government agencies with a foreign service cadre include USAID, DoS, USDA, and the DoC. Deployment overseas is a normal part of the foreign service role. Even where a department had a foreign service career track, civil service career employees can still be deployed on a case-by-case basis. Although foreign service career streams are designed around overseas deployment, the civil service career stream is not. For several offices, such as the DEA, overseas tours are a voluntary posting with a selection process.

The remainder of this section profiles each of the agencies and offices interviewed in turn. Although every attempt was made to discern the proportion and category of civilian employees whom the respective agencies and offices routinely deploy to high-stress postings, this information is not publicly available in some cases.

U.S. Department of Defense

DoD and the military services deploy civilian employees. Currently, civilians deploy in support of contingency operations in one of two ways: through agency-programmed requirements or through what

---

2 U.S. Code, Title 5, Government Organization and Employees, Section 2101, Civil Service; Armed Forces; Uniformed Services.

3 See, for example, U.S. Department of State, "Domestic/Civil Service," webpage, undated-a; U.S. Code, Title 22, Foreign Relations and Intercourse, Section 3902, Definitions.

4 U.S. Code, Title 22, Foreign Service and Intercourse, Chapter 52, Foreign Service; U.S. Department of State, "Foreign Service Officer," webpage, undated-b.

5 U.S. Code, Title 48, Federal Acquisition Regulations System, Section 37.104, Personal Services Contracts, pp. 733.

was known as the Civilian Expeditionary Workforce program in DoDD 1404.10 (now known as DoD expeditionary civilians). Service-specific agencies that routinely deploy civilians as part of their central missions, such as the Center for Army Analysis, the Army Audit Agency, and the U.S. Army Corps of Engineers, have long relied on programmed requirements to mobilize expeditionary civilians.

The vision for the Civilian Expeditionary Workforce program was first described in 2009 in DoDD 1404.10, *Civilian Expeditionary Workforce.*[6] This policy was issued as part of a statutory requirement in the National Defense Authorization Act for Fiscal Year (FY) 2007 with the goal of creating a standing cadre of 20,000 to 30,000 civilians who were prepared to mobilize quickly to fill high-demand roles for which there was a shortage of qualified uniformed personnel. DoDD 1404.10 outlined a program that would rely on a mix of military and civilian employees who would be "organized, ready, trained, cleared, and equipped in a manner that enhances their availability to mobilize and respond urgently to expeditionary requirements."[7] Ultimately, the Office of the Undersecretary of Defense for Civilian Personnel Policy, which oversaw the Civilian Expeditionary Workforce program office, made the decision to eliminate the cadre-based focus of the Civilian Expeditionary Workforce program and to focus on a more volunteer-based program aimed at meeting individual requirements for deployable DoD expeditionary civilians as requirements arose.

DoD civilian deployments often occur for a period of one year, which is longer than civilian deployments in the Department of Treasury, FEMA, and SIGAR, among other agencies. DoD-deployed civilians benefit from certain advantages over their civilian counterparts in other agencies in at least two ways. First, DoD expeditionary civilian workforce and the services' similar programs administer centralized pre- and post-deployment trainings at locations, including Camp Atterbury, Indiana; Fort Bliss, Texas; and Fort Dix, New Jersey. Centralized pre- and post-deployment trainings ensure a uniformity

---

[6] DoDD 1404.10, *DoD Civilian Expeditionary Workforce,* Washington, D.C.: U.S. Department of Defense, January 23, 2009.

[7] DoDD 1404.10, 2009, p. 2.

of experience and enable individuals to process their experiences with other deploying or deployed civilians. Second, upon their return, DoD civilian deployees typically return to bases and chains of command with substantial experience about post-deployment issues, while their non-DoD agency civilian counterparts do not.

Although DoD civilians typically deploy alongside uniformed service members, post-deployment decompression policies and practices differ from those offered to uniformed service members and more closely resemble the policies and practices on non-DoD federal agencies. Administratively, DoD civilians fall under Office of Personnel Management (OPM) guidelines for pay and benefits, including any treatment for post-deployment trauma or injury.

DoD civilians' post-deployment reintegration programs and processes are unique in several ways. As compared with uniformed service member deployments, DoD post-deployment programs are largely voluntary, in contrast with compulsory post-deployment programs for service members. DoD civilian deployees' completion of post-deployment programs and health assessments are not tied to future deployability and unit readiness as they are for U.S. service members. DoD civilians face different challenges than their uniformed deployed counterparts, especially with respect to a higher burden of proof for deployment-related injury claims through the Federal Employee Compensation Act (FECA) process than uniformed service members face with respect to continued treatment by DoD or the Department of Veterans Affairs.

Non-DoD Federal Agencies

U.S. Agency for International Development

Established in 1961, USAID's mission is to partner to end extreme poverty and promote resilient, democratic societies while advancing U.S. security and prosperity.[8] USAID works globally and its activities span a broad range, from education, health, and promoting gender equality to agriculture, food security, water, and sanitation.[9] USAID works in active conflict zones and in fragile and conflict-affected regions.

---

8 USAID, "Mission, Visions, Values," webpage, last updated February 2018.

9 USAID, "What We Do," webpage, last updated August 22, 2019a.

As of 2016, USAID had 1,677 foreign service and foreign service limited officers, and 376 U.S. PSCs deployed overseas; however, on average, USAID deployed approximately 1,800 staff to 80 countries overseas per year between FY 2001 and FY 2016.[10] Combined with other categories of employees, USAID had a total overseas workforce of 7,176 people in FY 2016.[11] USAID regulations state that the standard tour of duty for a foreign service officer is 24 months, but exceptionally challenging posts can be designated for one year.[12]

Within USAID, the research team interviewed individuals from both the OFDA and USAID Staff Care.[13] OFDA is responsible for leading and coordinating the U.S. government's response to disasters overseas. These events include rapid-onset disasters (such as earthquakes, volcanoes, and floods) and slow-onset crises (such as incidents brought about by drought and conflict). In response to major disasters, OFDA deploys DARTs to coordinate and manage the U.S. government response and work with local officials, the international community, and relief agencies. Depending on the number of DARTs deployed, OFDA could have up to 90 personnel deployed at any one time, although numbers are typically between 15 and 20 personnel deployed.[14]

The USAID Staff Care program provides resources to all USAID personnel deployed or at a home station, including non-U.S. citizen personnel hired overseas to perform USAID functions outside U.S. territory. The program has been in existence for five years and provides many services, including work-life coaching, child care subsidies, yoga, weight loss and nutritional counseling, crisis-response counsel-

10 RAND interview with USAID official, December 12, 2016; RAND interview with Treasury official, February 9, 2017; RAND interview with USAID official, January 19, 2017.

11 USAID, "Staffing Report to Congress," June 2016, p. 79.

12 USAID, Chapter 436, Foreign Service Assignments and Tours of Duty, *Automated Directives System*, October 18, 2011.

13 USAID, "Office of U.S. Foreign Disaster Assistance," webpage, last updated May 7, 2019a.

14 RAND interview with OFDA official, March 15, 2017.

ing, and other services in line with a traditional employee assistance program (EAP). To provide these services, USAID roughly allocates a total budget for Staff Care equal to approximately $800 per year per employee.[15] The office is staffed by 18 personnel across various employment categories of civil servants, foreign service officers, and PSCs.

U.S. Forest Service, Department of Agriculture

The U.S. Forest Service is part of the USDA. The Forest Service manages 193 million acres in 44 states and territories, representing 30 percent of all federally owned lands. The agency's mission is to sustain the health, diversity, and productivity of the nation's forests and grasslands to meet the needs of present and future generations.[16] The Forest Service employs approximately 28,603 scientists, administrators, and land managers, all of whom are civil servants and are not part of a foreign service cadre.[17] Within the Forest Service, there is a team of 20 to 40 personnel who support and deploy with USAID's OFDA when a disaster occurs. As part of this process, the Forest Service will stand up a team in both the Washington, D.C., office and one in the disaster-affected country.[18] The length of deployment to the affected country depends on the nature of the disaster, but it could last from weeks to months.[19]

U.S. Department of Commerce

The DoC's mission is to create the conditions for economic growth and opportunity by promoting innovation, entrepreneurship, competitiveness, and stewardship informed by world-class scientific research

---

15 RAND interview with USAID official, January 13, 2017.

16 USDA, U.S. Forest Service, "About the Agency," webpage, undated.

17 Data retrieved from March 2017 employment data cube using FedScope online tool, which can be found online at Office of Personnel Management, "FedScope: Federal Workforce Data," webpage, undated-b. Also see USDA, U.S. Forest Service, *Fiscal Year 2017 Budget Overview*, Washington, D.C., February 2016.

18 RAND interview with Forest Service official, April 13, 2017.

19 RAND interview with Forest Service official, April 13, 2017.

and information.[20] The DoC works across a wide variety of domestic and international commercial and business support and enablement areas, including trade and investment, innovation, the environment, and data. It has 12 bureaus and 46,566 employees across the United States and 218 in foreign countries.[21] The DoC has both a civil service and foreign service staff.[22] Foreign service staff typically deploy for a year or longer, while civil service employees deploy for a shorter duration, up to one year.[23]

U.S. Customs and Border Protection, Department of Homeland Security

CBP is part of DHS. CBP was established in 2003 with the mission of safeguarding U.S. borders, and "thereby protecting the public from dangerous people and materials while enhancing the Nation's global economic competitiveness by enabling legitimate trade and travel."[24] CBP is one of the largest law enforcement agencies in the world, with broad and diverse responsibilities "combining customs, immigration, border security, and agricultural protection" into one organization.[25] CBP has more than 60,000 employees, consisting of air and marine interdiction agents, border patrol agents, CBP officers, agriculture specialists, and professional staff.[26] At any given time, 1,000 CBP employees may be deployed abroad. Deployment lengths are typically two

---

[20] DoC, *U.S. Department of Commerce Strategic Plan, FY 2011–2016*, Washington, D.C., 2011.

[21] Data retrieved from March 2017 employment data cube using FedScope online tool, which can be found online at Office of Personnel Management, undated-b. FedScope only identifies employees in foreign countries who have that country as their official duty stations. It does not encompass employees who are there temporarily, therefore, it does not represent the entire deployed workforce.

[22] DoC, "About Commerce," webpage, undated.

[23] RAND interview with DOS official, January 23, 2017.

[24] CBP, "About CBP," webpage, last modified September 18, 2019a.

[25] CBP, 2019a.

[26] CBP, "Careers," webpage, last modified November 21, 2019b.

years, with the option to renew for an additional two years, and then for one final year.[27]

U.S. Federal Emergency Management Agency, Department of Homeland Security

As of March 2003, FEMA also falls under DHS. Established in 1979, FEMA's mission is to support citizens and first responders to build, sustain, and improve the national capability to prepare for, protect against, respond to, recover from, and mitigate all hazards.[28] FEMA has the responsibility for coordinating governmentwide relief efforts. FEMA deploys its staff domestically, but it does not deploy staff overseas. FEMA has ten regional field offices and a headquarters office. In 2017, it employed 4,150 staff (2,852 in its headquarters and 1,298 in the field offices).[29]

U.S. Office of International Engagement, Department of Homeland Security

DHS OIE replaced the Office of International Affairs in a 2015 reorganization of the DHS Policy Office.[30] The OIE engages with international partners outside the Western Hemisphere to further the DHS mission, represents the DHS in both international and domestic U.S. arenas, and coordinates the international efforts of other DHS components to ensure alignment with agency priorities.[31] Although OIE does not have a foreign service cadre, it routinely deploys personnel from other DHS components overseas for short-term deployments. Currently, the office has five individuals deployed, none in high-threat posts.[32]

---

27 RAND interview with CBP official, March 14, 2017.

28 FEMA, "About FEMA," webpage, last updated June 3, 2019.

29 DHS, *Federal Emergency Management Agency: Budget Overview, Fiscal Year 2018 Congressional Justification*, Washington, D.C., 2018.

30 Christian Beckner, "A Quiet But Notable Reorganization at DHS Headquarters," *Security Insights,* webpage, February 3, 2015.

31 DHS, Office of Strategy, Policy, and Plans, "The Office of International Engagement," webpage, last updated August 31, 2017.

32 RAND interview with OIE official, February 15, 2017.

U.S. Citizenship and Immigration Services, Department of Homeland Security

USCIS is the government department responsible for lawful immigration to the United States.[33] USCIS's mission is to unite immigrant families, provide for refugees, foster economic prosperity, promote citizenship, and protect the nation.[34] USCIS has 19,000 government employees and contractors working at 233 offices around the world.[35]

U.S. Immigration and Customs Enforcement, Department of Homeland Security

ICE was created in 2003 with a mission to protect the United States from cross-border crime and illegal immigration that threaten national security and public safety.[36] It focuses on three main areas of work: (1) immigration enforcement, (2) preventing terrorism, and (3) combating the illegal movement of people and goods.[37] It now has more than 20,000 employees, with offices in all 50 U.S. states and a presence in 48 foreign countries.[38]

U.S. Transportation Security Administration—Federal Air Marshal Service, Department of Homeland Security

FAMS is a U.S. federal law enforcement agency under the supervision of TSA. The DHS states that "the Federal Air Marshal Service deploys federal air marshals on U.S. aircraft worldwide, and conducts protection, response, detection and assessment activities in airports and other transportation systems."[39] It has 22 field offices domestically within the United States. FAMS does not publicly release information on the

---

[33] USCIS, "About Us," webpage, last updated March 6, 2018.

[34] USCIS, *USCIS Strategic Plan FY 2017–2021*, Washington D.C.: U.S. Department of Homeland Security, November 16, 2016, p. 1.

[35] USCIS, 2018.

[36] ICE, *Strategic Plan: 2016–2020*, Washington, D.C., January 2016, p. 10.

[37] ICE, "What We Do," webpage, last updated December 4, 2018.

[38] ICE, "History," webpage, last updated March 4, 2019.

[39] TSA, "About," webpage, undated.

number of law enforcement officers it employs or the number who are deployed at any one time.

U.S. Drug Enforcement Administration, Department of Justice

Part of the U.S. Department of Justice, the DEA mission is to

> . . . enforce the controlled substances laws and regulations of the United States and bring to the criminal and civil justice system of the United States, or any other competent jurisdiction, those organizations and principal members of organizations, involved in the growing, manufacture, or distribution of controlled substances appearing in or destined for illicit traffic in the United States; and to recommend and support non-enforcement programs aimed at reducing the availability of illicit controlled substances on the domestic and international markets.[40]

The DEA has 89 offices in 68 countries around the world.[41] It has 8,845 employees, approximately 800 to 1,000 of which are deployed overseas at any one time.[42] Among U.S. government agencies, the DEA has sole responsibility for coordinating and pursuing drug investigations abroad.[43] It does not have a foreign service cadre, and therefore relies on volunteers to staff its positions in foreign countries. Deployments vary in length. Federal law enforcement personnel can deploy for up to six years, whereas administration personnel do not have any limits on the length of time they can serve overseas.[44]

---

40 DEA, "Mission: DEA Mission Statement," webpage, undated.

41 U.S. Department of Justice, "Drug Enforcement Administration (DEA)," fact sheet, 2017.

42 RAND interview with DEA, January 19, 2017.

43 U.S. Department of Justice, 2017.

44 RAND interview with DEA official, January 19, 2017.

U.S. Department of State

The DoS mission is to

> . . . shape and sustain a peaceful, prosperous, just, and democratic world and foster conditions for stability and progress for the benefit of the American people and people everywhere. This mission is shared with the USAID, ensuring we have a common path forward in partnership as we invest in the shared security and prosperity that will ultimately better prepare us for the challenges of tomorrow.[45]

DoS supports the overseas activities of other U.S. government organizations, especially USAID. DoS has more than 270 embassies, consulates, and other posts in more than 180 countries. In 2016, DoS employed 14,490 foreign service officers and 13,699 civil servants. The DoS' civil service personnel are mostly domestically based in Washington, D.C.[46]

In addition to speaking to members of the DoS foreign service and civil service staffs, the research team also interviewed staff from the DoS Bureau of Medical Services and the DoS FSI. The Bureau of Medical Services manages and operates the DoS worldwide medical program serving more than 70,000 U.S. government employees and their family members from more than 75 federal agencies working overseas.[47] The FSI provides the full range of training and education to all professional cadres of the DoS.[48]

---

[45] DoS, *Agency Financial Report, Fiscal Year 2016*, Washington, D.C.: U.S. Department of State, Bureau of Public Affairs, November 2016, p. 7.

[46] DoS, *Congressional Budget Justification: Department of State, Foreign Operations, and Related Programs, Fiscal Year 2018*, Washington, D.C., May 23, 2017b, p. 20.

[47] DoS, 2017b, p. 78.

[48] DoS, 2017b, p. 60.

U.S. Department of the Treasury

The U.S. Department of the Treasury's mission is to:

> Maintain a strong economy and create economic and job opportunities by promoting conditions that enable economic growth and stability at home and abroad and manage the U.S. Government's finances and resources effectively.[49]

The Treasury Department has a wide range of responsibilities, from providing economic advice to the President to ensuring the financial security of the United States by maintaining systems that are critical to the financial infrastructure. The Treasury Department has several operating bureaus to carry out its work, including the Internal Revenue Service (IRS) and the U.S. Mint. The Treasury employs 86,497 full-time equivalent direct staff. The IRS employs the vast majority of these (77,925).[50] The vast majority of Treasury Department staff do not deploy internationally, but it does have 15 to 20 attaché positions at U.S. embassies and missions overseas, and it will occasionally send staff to international organizations.

U.S. Federal Agency Law, Policy, and Guidance Related to Civilian Post-Deployment Reintegration

DoD policy lays forth the expectations for civilian deployments and, in part, for civilian post-deployment reintegration. When deploying, DoDD 1400.31, *DoD Civilian Work Force Contingency and Emergency Planning and Execution,* outlines the expectations and chain of command for the DoD civilian work force.[51] Although post-deployment reintegration is not a specific emphasis of DoDD 1400.31, the policy focuses on ensuring an "appropriate state of readiness" across the DoD

---

[49] U.S. Department of Treasury, "Role of the Treasury," webpage, undated.

[50] U.S. Department of Treasury, "FY 2018, Executive Summary: Congressional Justification For Appropriations And Annual Performance Report And Plan," 2018.

[51] DoDD 1400.31, *DoD Civilian Work Force Contingency and Emergency Planning and Execution*, Washington, D.C.: U.S. Department of Defense, 1995.

civilian workforce.[52] The policy assigns responsibility for establishing "broad personnel recruitment, training, administration, utilization, retention, and placement policies and assumptions" of deployed civilian personnel to the Under Secretary of Defense for Personnel and Readiness. Because successful reintegration might affect the retention and readiness of civilian personnel who deploy multiple times, civilian post-deployment reintegration might benefit from further consideration by the Under Secretary of Defense for Personnel and Readiness under the authorities laid out in DoDD 1400.31.

DoDI 1400.32, *DoD Civilian Work Force Contingency and Emergency Planning Guidelines and Procedures*, assigns the responsibility for ensuring that deployed civilians receive the necessary training, processing, and support in the preparation for deployment and throughout deployment.[53] Although the instruction provides detailed requirements for civilian pre-deployment and deployment practices, it does not acknowledge post-deployment reintegration.

DoDI 6490.03 provides DoD policy for deployment health to include DoD civilians. The policy requires that all deploying government civilians are briefed prior to deployment on any potential health and safety hazards, including potential outcomes of operational stress.[54] The DoDI further provides for "follow-up of deployment-related exposures, injuries, or illness," with the specific proviso that, for DoD civilians, post-deployment follow-up is "consistent with workers compensation laws," and that any follow-up medical care within a military treatment facility is authorized.

Meanwhile, non-DoD federal agencies follow the lead of two overarching structures: (1) the DoS under the U.S. Embassy Chief of Mission jurisdiction when deployed in country, and (2) the OPM for stateside administrative policies and procedures.

---

[52] DoDD 1400.31, 1995, p. 2.

[53] DoDI 1400.32, *DoD Civilian Work Force Contingency and Emergency Planning Guidelines and Procedures*, Washington, D.C.: U.S. Department of Defense, 1995, p. 3.

[54] DoDI 6490.03, 2019.

U.S. Department of State

The majority of the non-DoD federal agencies included in this study deploy their civilian staff under the U.S. Embassy Chief of Mission jurisdiction; managers from these agencies therefore indicated in interviews that they rely upon DoS policies and guidelines by default. Indeed, interviewees from five of the seven agencies interviewed, including DoS, stated that it was easier to follow DoS policies than to create their own departmental variations.[55]

Principal among DoS guidance documents are the *Foreign Affairs Manual* and *Foreign Affairs Handbook*, which are the source documents for DoS deployment policies and procedures. More specifically, the DoS has published information about the Deployment Stress Management Program (DSMP), which resides in the Bureau of Medical Services. It supports the psychological health of DoS employees during a deployment and works to integrate stress-management training, stress prevention and detection, and consultation on treatment after a deployment across DoS.[56]

The DSMP is intended to help DoS and USAID personnel both deploying to and returning from high-threat posts. It "offers prevention, intervention, assessment, consultation, education and referral services covering the spectrum of the deployment cycle."[57] DSMP offers a high-stress assignment outbrief, which is mandatory for DoS employees returning from specific high-stress posts, encouraged for employees returning from all other high-stress posts, and open to other employees of DoS or other federal agencies.[58]

---

55 RAND interviews with Treasury officials, February 9, 2017, and March 16, 2017; RAND interview with DHS officials, February 15, 2017, and March 14, 2017; RAND interviews with DOS officials, February 8–9, 2017; RAND interview with DoC official, February 15, 2017; RAND interview with Forest Service official, April 13, 2017.

56 DoS, "Deployment Stress Management Program (DSMP)," *Foreign Affairs Manual*, Vol. 16, Chapter 440, March 2019a; DoS, "Purpose," *Foreign Affairs Manual*, Vol. 16, Chapter 441, March 2019b.

57 DoS, Bureau of Medical Services, "Deployment Stress Management Program," webpage, undated.

58 DoS, "High Stress Assignment Outbrief," webpage, undated-b.

At least one agency represented in our interviews uses DoS policies as a baseline and then augments those policies with its own agency-specific policies. USAID employs this approach and uses the Automated Directives System to provide guidance that governs operations and programs.[59] Several USAID directives are relevant to decompression, including those on "Leave," the "Overseas Employment Program," and "Awards and other Recognition Programs."[60] Additionally, USAID offers the Staff Care program to its employees. However, policy governing Staff Care is not publicly available, and there is limited information about it on the USAID Staff Care website.[61]

With limited established civilian redeployment and reintegration policy and guidance, federal agencies' EAPs appear to be the primary means through which non-DoD federal agency civilians receive care or support for deployment-related or reintegration issues. EAPs vary in the breadth and diversity of their offerings. However, in general, an EAP is a "voluntary, work-based program that offers free and confidential assessments, short-term counseling, referrals, and follow-up services to employees who have personal and/or work-related problems."[62] Examples include access to telehealth counseling sessions for difficulties at work or home, as well as access to alcohol counseling. Federal Occupational Health (FOH) is a service unit within the Program Support Center of the Department of Health and Human Services, and was created in 1946 with an amendment to the Public Health Service Act.[63] It provides occupational health services to more than 360 federal agencies and offices under the auspices of the Economy Act,[64] which

59 USAID, "About the ADS," webpage, last updated October 28, 2013.

60 USAID, "ADS Series 400," webpage, last updated September 24, 2019a.

61 USAID, "Staff Care," webpage, last updated September 17, 2019b.

62 OPM, "What Is an Employee Assistance Program (EAP)?" webpage, undated-d.

63 U.S. Department of Health and Human Services, Program Support Center, Federal Occupational Health, "About FOH," webpage, undated-a; U.S. Department of Health and Human Services, Federal Occupational Health, "The Interagency Agreement," webpage, undated-b.

64 U.S. Department of Health and Human Services, Program Support Center, Federal Occupational Health, "Doing Business with FOH and Interagency Agreements (IAAs),"

allows federal agencies to procure goods or services from another federal agency.[65]

The services that FOH offers include EAPs, which cover more than 700,000 federal employees and their family members.[66] Although federal law requires agencies to provide services to help employees with a variety of issues, to include alcohol and drug abuse problems,[67] the law notably does *not* require agencies to provide "a health service program to promote and maintain the physical and mental fitness of employees under its jurisdiction."[68]

Office of Personnel Management

OPM provides the overall administrative structure for all deployed federal civilians. OPM provides specific guidelines surrounding issues of pay and benefits. Although policies may differ across agencies, OPM works with DoD and DoS to align policies and processes across the federal government where possible.[69] OPM policies ensure that deployed civilians receive enhanced entitlements during deployment, including an increase in the ceiling on their annual leave accrual while deployed (360 hours as compared with the standard 240 hours allotted to federal employees working stateside).[70]

The 2012 National Defense Authorization Act established a requirement that the heads of all federal agencies were responsible for creating a structured Post-Combat Case Coordinator (PCCC) role

---

webpage, undated-b.

65 U.S. Code, Title 31, Money and Finance, Section 1535, Agency Agreements.

66 U.S. Department of Health and Human Services, Federal Occupational Health, "Employee Assistance Program," webpage, undated-a.

67 Barbara Haga, "Employee Participation in Employee Assistance Programs," Federal Employment Law Training Group, undated.

68 U.S. Code, Title 5, Government Organization and Employees, Section 7901, Health Service Programs.

69 John Berry, "Deployed Federal Civilians: Advancing Security and Opportunity in Afghanistan," before the Subcommittee on Oversight of Government Management, the Federal Workforce, and the District of Columbia Committee on Homeland Security and Governmental Affairs, U.S. Senate, Washington, D.C., April 14, 2010.

70 Berry, 2010.

within their agencies,[71] for which OPM provides the framework and guidelines.[72] The PCCC role was designed to serve as an agency point of contact for individuals who suffered any injury, disability, or illness as a result of their work in a combat zone. The PCCC role is intended to assist employees in the process of properly documenting all supporting evidence for their claims, which might include pre-deployment health assessments, incident reports, and medical records.[73] OPM suggests that, when possible, the PCCC role should be filled by the agency's Office of Workers' Compensation Programs (OWCP) coordinator to streamline the benefits process and that agencies with larger numbers of deployed civilians should consider training multiple PCCCs within their organizations.

The dearth of specific guidance—at least in the public domain—on various aspects of civilian post-deployment reintegration across much of the U.S. federal agency community is in stark contrast to the detailed guidance and policy seen across both DoD and the services on military post-deployment reintegration, which is elaborated in Chapter Two. To the extent that well-defined policy forms a basis for effective practice, this speaks to a need for the respective U.S. federal agencies deploying civilians to define and specify their own individual guidance regarding post-deployment reintegration as a first step to ensuring improved and systematized reintegration programs, activities, and overall practice.

Federal Agency Civilian Post-Deployment Reintegration Practices

Categorizing post-deployment activities amongst the organizations represented by the individuals in the interview sample (see Table 3.1), illustrates both the variation and range of post-deployment reintegra-

---

71 Public Law 112-81, National Defense Authorization Act (NDAA) for Fiscal Year 2012, December 31, 2011; U.S. Code, Title 5, Government Organization and Employees, Section 7906, Services of Post-Combat Case Coordinators.

72 OPM, "Guidelines: Post-Combat Case Coordinator," Washington, D.C., 2013.

73 OPM, 2013.

Table 3.1
Breakdown of Formal Post-Deployment Reintegration Activities and Programs Across U.S. Federal Agencies

Organization	Administrative Outprocessing	Health Assessments	Decompression Activity	Post-Deployment Leave	Resiliency Training	Recognition	Reintegration Activities	Post-Trauma Practices	Personnel Tracking
Non-DoD Federal Civilians									
PSC	■								
DHS OIE	■	■		■					
U.S. Department of Commerce	■		■						
U.S. Department of Treasury	■			■					
Federal Air Marshals Service	■	■		■				■	
U.S. Forest Service	■			■					■
DEA	■		■	■	■	■	■	■	■

Table 3.1—Continued

Organization	Administrative Outprocessing	Health Assessments	Decompression Activity	Post-Deployment Leave	Resiliency Training	Recognition	Reintegration Activities	Post-Trauma Practices	Personnel Tracking
Customs and Border Protection (CBP)									
USAID									
DoS									
DoD Civilians									
SIGAR									
Department of the Navy Expeditionary Civilian Program									
Department of the Air Force Expeditionary Civilian Program									

Table 3.1—Continued

Organization	Administrative Outprocessing	Health Assessments	Decompression Activity	Post-Deployment Leave	Resiliency Training	Recognition	Reintegration Activities	Post-Trauma Practices	Personnel Tracking
DoD Expeditionary Civilian Program Office	Yes	Yes	Some form of activity	Unknown	Some form of activity	Unknown	Some form of activity	Some form of activity	Some form of activity
DoD Uniformed Service Members									
DoD Uniformed Service Members	Yes	Yes	Yes	Yes	Yes	Yes	Yes	Yes	Yes

NOTE: Data reflects coded results of interviews and may be subject to some error because of interviewee perceptions. Because the sample size was relatively small, the results may not be entirely indicative of actual agency practices; in addition, only information for agencies where we had data were included. In cases where interview results were conflicting, coding favored inclusion of an activity in the results. DHS = U.S. Department of Homeland Security; DoS = U.S. Department of State; PSC = personal services contractors; OIE = Office of International Engagement; SIGAR = Special Inspector General for Afghanistan Reconstruction; USAID = U.S. Agency for International Development.

Yes | No | Some form of activity | Unknown

tion practices performed across the non-DoD federal agencies studied here, and provides some indication of where gaps may exist.[74] When reviewing these findings, it is critical to keep in mind that they are based on a limited number of interviews and may be subject to some error. Nonetheless, these findings have utility in providing general insights into federal agency civilian post-deployment reintegration practices.

The research team coded the interviews as follows: When an interviewee stated the service was provided by the organization, the category was coded as "yes"; when an interviewee mentioned that some, but not all, of the relevant activities were conducted in the category, the category was coded as "some form of activity"; when no activity was indicated, the category was coded as "no." When incongruities existed between statements from multiple personnel interviewed from the same organization, the research team coded as "unknown" any activities that even one interviewee provided.

Of note, there is a strong correlation between the number of deployees within an agency and the sophistication of reintegration programming. Figure 3.1 depicts the distribution of civilians deployed overseas by department or agency. The correlation indicates that, as the demand for deployed civilians increases across agencies, those agencies may benefit from examining the policies, practices, and procedures of agencies that regularly deploy large numbers of civilians.

The provision of current civilian post-deployment reintegration concepts and practices appears to also vary based on the type of authority under which an individual is hired. Relevant categories of civilian employment across U.S. non-DoD federal agencies include civil service, foreign service, PSCs, reservists,[75] intermittent staff, government service employees, and local national personnel. Relevant categories of civilian deployment across DoD include civil service, PSCs, and

---

[74] During the interview process the research team used Human Subject Protections protocols. These protocols were developed and used in accordance with the appropriate statutes and DoD regulations governing Human Subject Protections.

[75] Note that the term *reservist* here refers to non-DoD federal agency reservists, who deploy in civilian status. U.S. military reserve component members are not within the study's scope, because they deploy in uniformed status.

Figure 3.1
Estimated Numbers of Deployed Civilians Annually (Highest Estimate)

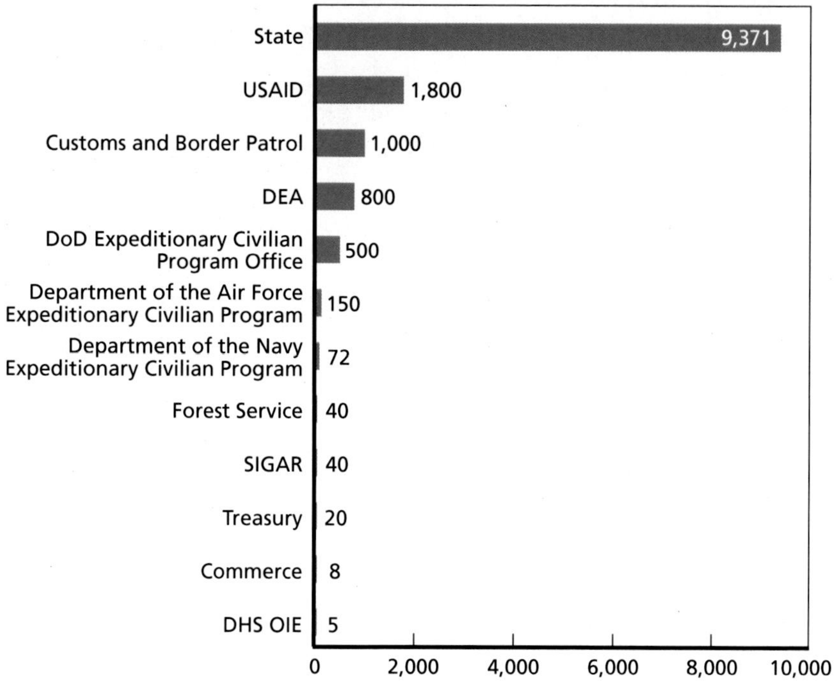

intermittent staff. Of note, PSCs typically receive no post-deployment reintegration programming other than administrative outprocessing, which would logically be a necessity at the end of a contract's duration. Therefore, in many ways, PSCs fall into a crack in the systems of the agencies in question, and policymakers in these agencies may want to pay special attention to the programming provided to these contractors.

Although Table 3.1 shows that all agencies engage in some post-deployment activities, there is little consistency across federal agencies included in this study. Of the categories of reintegration activity considered here, interviewees most commonly reported experience with administrative outprocessing; interviewees also frequently reported experience with post-deployment leave as a type of reintegration practice. Most interviewees indicated that practices in the areas of decompression programs, recognition and awards, community and family reintegration, and post-trauma activities tended to occur only in some moderate form or not at all. DoS and DEA performed post-deployment reintegration practices across the largest number of categories (six categories for DEA and six categories for DoS), and the Department of the Treasury, DoC, and the SIGAR performed post-deployment reintegration practices across the fewest number of categories (two each).[76]

In general, interviewees stated that their organizations use their own staff processes in reintegrating personnel who return from a deployment, and do not look to the military for promising practices. However, strong U.S. military precedents and some evidentiary basis do exist for the key categories of programs mentioned above that are (with several exceptions) noticeably absent for U.S. federal civilians returning from deployments: decompression, community and family reintegration, and post-trauma practices.

Each category of reintegration practice and relevant agency activities are elaborated in further detail below.

Administrative Outprocessing

All organizations reported using some form of administrative outprocessing,[77] which generally took the form of an outbrief in country and some administrative paperwork. This was not the only form

---

[76] It should be noted that PSCs only performed administrative out processing. However, these personnel work across agencies and are a category of worker, not an agency (see Figure 3.1).

[77] RAND interview with non-DoD federal official, March 14, 2017; RAND interviews with non-DoD federal officials, February 6 and 15, 2017; RAND interviews with non-DoD federal officials, November 22, 2016, January 12 and 23, 2017; RAND interview with non-DoD official, January 31, 2017; RAND interviews with non-DoD federal officials, February 21, 2017, and March 6 and 17, 2017; RAND interview with non-DoD federal official, February 15, 2017; RAND interview with non-DoD federal official, February 23, 2017; RAND interviews with non-DoD officials, February 24, 2017, and March 16, 2017; RAND interviews with non-DoD federal officials, November 22, 2016, and December 12, 2016; RAND interview with non-DoD federal official, January 17, 2017; RAND interview with non-DoD federal official, February 17, 2017; RAND interview with non-DoD federal official, February 15, 2017.

of administrative outprocessing, though, and ten interviewees said that they received this outbrief upon return to the home offices. Of those interviewed, 18 identified reintegration activities as being largely administrative in nature,[78] and eight identified that they had gone through the process.[79] However, other than in DoS, no offices or personnel within human resources in any of the agencies studied were dedicated to taking responsibility for or managing post-deployment administrative outprocessing. Such outprocessing was, in almost every case, handled through regular human resources channels and processes.

Reintegration process and practices in DoD civilian organizations are largely administrative in nature and more frequently focused on the pre-deployment process rather than post-deployment reintegration, which is indicated in interviews with Civilian Expeditionary Workforce managers and human resources offices within DoD and the services. Representatives from DoD, the Department of the Air Force, and the Department of the Navy all expressed their role in the development of pre- and post-deployment checklists for deploying and deployed civilians to streamline administrative processes.[80] Additionally, DoD and service civilian deployment managers focus much of their attention to issues surrounding pay and benefits paperwork. Although the offices place less

---

[78] RAND interviews with non-DoD federal officials, February 6 and 15, 2017; RAND interview with non-DoD federal official, January 31, 2017; RAND interview with non-DoD federal official, January 23, 2017; RAND interview with non-DoD federal officials, February 21, 2017, and March 6 and 17, 2017; RAND interview with non-DoD federal official, February 15, 2017; RAND interview with non-DoD federal official, February 23, 2017; RAND interviews with non-DoD federal officials, February 9 and 24, 2017; RAND interview with non-DoD federal officials, November 22, 2016, December 12, 2016, and January 13 and 19, 2017; RAND interview with non-DoD federal official, January 17, 2017; RAND interview with non-DoD federal official, February 17, 2017.

[79] RAND interview with non-DoD federal officials, February 6 and 17, 2017, RAND interview with non-DoD federal official, February 23, 2017; RAND interviews with non-DoD federal officials, February 24, 2017, and March 16, 2017; RAND interviews with non-DoD federal officials, November 22, 2016, and December 12, 2016; RAND interview with non-DoD federal official, February 17, 2017.

[80] RAND interview with DoD manager, February 26, 2019; RAND interview with DoD manager, March 5, 2019; RAND interview with DoD manager, January 28, 2019; RAND interview with Department of the Air Force manager, February 26, 2019; RAND interview with Navy civilian deployment manager, March 5, 2019.

emphasis on post-deployment reintegration processes, managers note the necessity of managing pay and benefit timelines and paperwork so as to prevent any future financial penalty to the deployed individual upon return.[81] Although DoD and service offices provide limited services directly to civilians post-deployment, the offices do focus on connecting civilians to existing services when necessary after deployment. For example, even though DoD does not provide post-deployment health-related compensation to the expeditionary civilian workforce, offices will assist deployed civilians in filing workers' compensation claims under FECA to ensure they receive the appropriate benefits.[82]

These administrative outprocessing practices are in contrast to military processes, where all organizations conduct a more-thorough outprocessing and have well-established processes. Although each military organization conducts outprocessing somewhat differently, most require personnel to go through multiple activities, and almost all provide service members with a formal checklist of activities to be completed. Each activity is monitored to ensure personnel complete each stage before they can formally outprocess. This is to ensure completion of all paperwork and to allow for accounting of all equipment and updating of all benefits and entitlements. The administrative requirements for uniformed service members are also tied to their future deployability and unit readiness. No similar requirement exists for deployed federal civilians.

Health Assessments

None of the civilian agencies interviewed had any form of mandatory post-deployment health assessment for deployed staff, though five interviewees reported having some type of medical check-up upon return from a deployment.[83] For those DoS personnel leaving a high-stress

---

81 RAND interview with DoD civilian expeditionary human resources manager, January 28, 2019.

82 RAND interview with Department of the Air Force manager, February 26, 2019.

83 RAND interview with non-DoD federal official, February 15, 2017, RAND interview with non-DoD federal official, December 20, 2016; RAND interview with non-DoD federal official, March 16, 2017; RAND interview with non-DoD federal official, January 31, 2017.

environment, the DoS FSI does have a mandatory briefing providing information about PTSD and the effects of stress.[84] Within DoS, the Bureau of Medical Services provided medical support to personnel but could not mandate that people attend a medical assessment following redeployment. Across departments, 17 interviewees noted that if deployees wanted to access health care following a deployment, they would either have to actively seek help or access it through their own insurance.[85] Additionally, 12 interviewees identified that EAPs were the main source of post-deployment medical assistance for deployees; however, the specific services provided varied across agencies, offices, and particular EAPs.[86]

USAID does have a Staff Care program available to all categories of employed personnel—to include personnel hired in another country working on a USAID project—that provides access to some medical and mental health services.[87] While all USAID personnel have access to the program, it could be used more.[88] There are several reasons personnel might not use Staff Care, which is noted by one interviewee who said that, "talking about Staff Care isn't done, it's kind of stigmatized."[89] While this may be the case, four of the five USAID

---

[84] RAND interview with DoS official, December 20, 2017.

[85] RAND interview with non-DoD federal officials, February 6 and 15, 2017; RAND interview with non-DoD federal officials, December 20, 2016, and January 8, 12, and 23, 2017; RAND interviews with non-DoD federal officials, February 21, 2017, and March 6, 2017; RAND interview with non-DoD federal official, February 23, 2017; RAND interview with non-DoD federal official, February 9, 2017; RAND interviews with non-DoD federal officials, November 22, 2016, December 12, 2016, and January 13, 2017; RAND interview with non-DoD federal official, January 17, 2017; RAND interview with non-DoD federal official, November 21, 2016; RAND interview with non-DoD federal official, February 17, 2017.

[86] RAND interviews with non-DoD federal official, February 15, 2017; RAND interview with non-DoD federal official, January 31, 2017; RAND interview with non-DoD federal official, February 9, 2017; RAND interview with non-DoD federal official, January 17, 2017; RAND interview with non-DoD federal official, February 21, 2017; RAND interview with non-DoD federal official, December 20, 2016.

[87] RAND interview with non-DoD federal official, January 13, 2017.

[88] RAND interview with non-DoD federal official, January 13, 2017.

[89] RAND interview with non-DoD federal official, November 22, 2017.

personnel interviewed were positive about some or all aspects of Staff Care.[90] One interviewee noted that, "For USAID, it's a big step in the right direction that they have . . . Staff Care, the fact that they have these expeditionary teams to treat Foreign Service Nationals if something happens in a country, and the fact that Staff Care is accessible to all types of employees is positive."[91]

DoD policy for post-deployment health assessments is more comprehensive and includes multiple processes to document exposure to both high-stress incidents and potential exposure to harmful environmental factors. DoD-employed physical and mental health professionals carefully follow DoD service members screening processes for any type of post-deployment health issues. Individuals identified as having been exposed to these types of events are often referred to appropriate medical treatment options. While there are limits to military health assessments, which are indicated by at least two studies,[92] the services are attempting to destigmatize PTSD and other mental health issues. These assessments can at least be a first step toward providing deployees with assistance, and all of the individual military services have implemented a mental health assessment, which is mandated by DoD.[93]

Decompression Programs

As noted in Chapter Two, the U.S. military makes use of third-party sites for decompression after deployment. To facilitate post-deployment decompression for uniformed service members and civilians, the Air Force established the DTC with a TLD center at Ramstein Air Base, Germany in 2010. The center offers those returning from a combat

---

90 RAND interviews with non-DoD federal officials, November 22, 2016, December 12, 2016, and January 13 and 19, 2017.

91 RAND interview with non-DoD federal official, January 13, 2017.

92 Warner et al., 2011, p. 1065; Roberto J. Rona, Howard Burdett, Mizanur Khondoker, Melanie Chesnokov, Kevin Green, David Pernet, Norman Jones, Neil Greenberg, Simon Wessely, and Nicola T. Fear, "Post-Deployment Screening for Mental Disorders and Tailored Advice About Help-Seeking in the UK Military: A Cluster Randomised Controlled Trial," *Lancet*, Vol. 389, No. 10077, April 8, 2017.

93 DoD, 2013.

zone the opportunity to decompress before reintegrating into their pre-deployment routines.[94] Interviewees from DoD and the Navy stated that no formal process exists for civilian post-deployment decompression within their services. However, the interviewees noted that, if necessary, civilians could access the DTC with the support of their deployment command.

Ten interviewees indicated that reintegration was an important issue and that civilian decompression programs could be useful. There is recognition among the U.S. federal civilian deployee and management populations that military decompression activities have generated promising practices that civilian agencies could leverage. One interviewee mentioned, "As a system, we're becoming more and more militarized, yet we haven't kept up pace with best practices for mental health."[95]

Of the non-DoD agencies included in this study, DoS, DEA, DoC, and USAID identified decompression activities.[96] The most prominent activities reside at the DoS FSI, which holds post-deployment courses and briefings for both DoS and USAID employees. Outside DoS, DEA was one of the few agencies interviewed that was engaged in any decompression activities through its development of a new post-deployment decompression and family reintegration program.[97] In September 2016, the DEA ran a trial of this program for staff returning from overseas deployments. The program lasted three days at a DEA office and included the participation of both staff who had been deployed to high-risk locations and military reservists who had returned from deployment. The course included the participation of spouses and was, at the time of writing, still a nascent program based solely on voluntary participation of returned deployees. The three-day program included lectures and seminars on relevant topics, including post-deployment health issues and tips for readjusting to the domestic workplace. According to the program

---

[94] For an analysis of the effectiveness of the DTC, see Schell et al., 2016.

[95] RAND interview with non-DoD federal official, February 8, 2017.

[96] RAND interview with non-DoD federal official, January 31, 2017; RAND interview with DoS official, January 12, 2017.

[97] RAND interview with non-DoD federal official, January 19, 2017.

organizers within DEA, the program was very well received by participants and the DEA intends to run two of these decompression programs in 2020, hoping to reach a bigger audience.[98]

Outside DoS and DEA programs, and despite the theoretical ability for civilians to proceed through military TLD sites as noted earlier, none of the interviewees reported proceeding through any type of formal decompression similar to the programs available to U.S. military service members.[99] This is unsurprising, because most U.S. non-DoD federal agencies do not have any form of formal decompression for their returning deployees. As a normal part of leave or as part of return travel, at least one interviewee was able to arrange a layover in a third-party country.[100] However, such layovers are not the same as the organized use of a third-party location for decompression, in the vein of the military TLD programs. This is due in part to the fact that civilians tend to deploy as individual augmentees, whereas military service members deploy more frequently, though not always, in units. It is therefore relatively straightforward to send military units through TLD sites; identification and utilization of such sites for individual civilian use would require further coordination and has yet to be done. For most civilians, post-deployment leave or rest and recuperation acted as a de facto form of decompression—although to our knowledge, there is not yet any evidence to support its utility.

Some services use TLD more than others and place greater emphasis on the practice. However, existing studies on the effectiveness of TLD does not find benefit with the practice; therefore, caution should be taken in generating TLD locations based on military practices. Any consideration of adapting TLD programs for a civilian audience should include a plan to comprehensively pilot-test such a practice.

Post-Deployment Leave

Even if they had no other form of post-deployment policy or practice, interviewees from six offices indicated that their respective orga-

---

[98] RAND interview with non-DoD federal official, January 31, 2017.

[99] RAND interview with non-DoD federal official, March 15, 2017.

[100] RAND interview with non-DoD federal official, January 31, 2017.

nizations provide some form of post-deployment leave.[101] This was one of only two consistent post-deployment activities that were identified during the course of this research. The amount of leave varied between offices, and, in general, was dependent on the length of time deployed, type of employment contract, and the subsequent needs of the agency or office in question. Several organizations allocated additional leave for administrative purposes, with eight interviewees stating that they were provided extra leave time for such a reason.

Other agencies did not stop personnel from taking leave, although they also did not encourage the use of leave. For example, one interviewee stated that his home office was understaffed and that taking leave would hinder his colleagues; thus, the interviewee did not take any leave.[102] Attitudes and experiences varied with regard to the amount of leave to which people were entitled, and the amount of leave they desired or were encouraged to take. At least one interviewee cited examples of multiple departments that encouraged staff to take leave.[103]

Formalizing a deployment-related mandatory leave policy could be considered to ensure that civilians take leave upon returning from a deployment. Again, it is important to note that research on the utility of post-deployment leave and the effects of timing and length is recommended before implementing these policies. While most non-DoD federal agencies likely have a limit on the amount of leave time that employees may accrue, it would be reasonable to alter an organization's leave policy to increase leave time, specifically in cases of civilian deployment. This would be more in line with military practices, where leave is encouraged after a deployment.

---

[101] RAND interview with non-DoD federal official, March 14, 2017; RAND interviews with non-DoD federal officials, December 29, 2016, and January 12, 2017; RAND interview with non-DoD federal official, March 17, 2017; RAND interview with non-DoD federal official, February 15, 2017; RAND interview with non-DoD federal official, February 23, 2017; RAND interviews with non-DoD federal officials, February 9 and 24, 2017, and March 16, 2017.

[102] RAND interview with non-DoD federal official, March 15, 2017.

[103] RAND interview with non-DoD federal official, February 24, 2017.

Recognition and Awards

There were three examples of recognition in our interviews of people deploying to high-stress and high-threat environments, they received awards beyond those for gallantry or decorations for exceptional service. However, employees do appreciate awards recognizing their service while deployed, as noted by one interviewee:

> I was very pleased with both Treasury and State. We didn't do an event, but I did get a nice financial reward from Treasury and a nice recognition of service from the State Department, which was unique, because they don't usually give out awards to non-State employees. Both kudos happened soon after I came back.[104]

Overall, 20 interviewees mentioned the lack of recognition upon redeployment.[105] The aforementioned 2010 Office of Inspector General report specifically identified this issue as an area for improvement.[106]

Juxtaposed against this approach are the service practices of providing awards to almost all personnel who deploy. Whether a campaign medal for going to a specific country or region, or an award for performing duties in a hazardous area, the military services are exemplars of recognizing deployed service. Although only one agency cited examples of formal awards and recognition, prior RAND research has found that this is an effective practice to enhance recruitment and utilization of civilian deployees, at least among foreign defense organizations.[107]

---

[104] RAND interview with non-DoD federal official, March 16, 2017.

[105] RAND interviews with non-DoD federal officials, February 6 and 15, 2017; RAND interview with non-DoD federal officials, January 31, 2017; RAND interview with non-DoD federal officials, November 21, 2016; RAND interviews with non-DoD federal officials, February 21, 2017, and March 6 and 17, 2017; RAND interview with non-DoD federal official, March 15, 2017; RAND interview with non-DoD federal official, February 23, 2017; RAND interviews with non-DoD federal officials, February 9 and 24, 2017; RAND interviews with non-DoD federal officials, November 22, 2016, December 12, 2016, and January 13 and 19, 2017; RAND interview with non-DoD federal official, January 17, 2017; RAND interview with non-DoD federal official, January 17, 2017.

[106] DoS, Broadcasting Board of Governors, Office of Inspector General, 2010, p. 29.

[107] Dunigan, Schwille, et al., 2016; Dunigan, Everingham, et al., 2016.

Civilian agencies should consider adopting the service approaches to awards and recognition for those civilians who volunteer for high-stress and high-threat deployments, raising awareness of such deployments across the agency and civilian deployees' morale. Although not every deployee needs a medal or special recognition to adequately perform his or her job, such recognition would be one way to partially ease the transition back to civilian life following a deployment.

Community and Family Reintegration Activities

Whereas ten interviewees identified reintegration activities as being important, 55 percent of the entire interview sample (20 of 36) mentioned that reintegration activities were lacking upon redeployment. Interviewees also spoke of a tension and lack of mutual understanding between those who have deployed and those who have not. Six interviewees from five different organizations reported that when they returned to their home offices and resumed their domestic job, people in the domestic offices did not understand some of the challenges they had experienced in reintegrating after deployment. This lack of mutual understanding made reintegration more difficult for the deployees in question.[108]

In contrast to civilian personnel, the military and veteran communities (outside the formal organizations and chain of command) have made extensive use of informal or voluntary networks and groups for peer support. Examples of these include Facebook groups, listservs, reunions and meetings, and voluntary activities or support. Among civilians deployees interviewed, 15 interviewees responded that they were unaware of any form of informal or voluntary networks, groups, or other support activities.[109]

---

108 RAND interviews with non-DoD federal officials, January 12 and 23, 2017; RAND interview with non-DoD federal official, December 12, 2017; RAND interview with non-DoD federal official, February 23, 2017; RAND interview with non-DoD federal official, February 9, 2017; RAND interview with non-DoD federal official, February 17, 2017.

109 RAND interviews with non-DoD federal officials, February 21, 2017, and March 6, 2017; RAND interview with non-DoD federal officials, February 9 and 24, 2017; RAND interview with non-DoD federal official, February 15, 2017; RAND interview with non-DoD federal official, February 15, 2017; RAND interviews with non-DoD federal officials,

At a minimum, federal agencies deploying civilians should consider the more-informal methods that service members and veterans have adopted to help personnel reintegrate upon redeployment. An easy way to do this would be to connect those who have previously deployed with those personnel who have recently returned from a deployment. Programs (such as the YRRP) that provide counseling, referrals for treatment, family activities, and relationship workshops should also be considered and could possibly be combined and synergized across several federal agencies for returned civilian deployees.

Post-Trauma Practices

Apart from DoS, few other departments offer any form of post-deployment stress control training. The DoS FSI Transition Center runs the High Stress Assignment Outbrief Program, primarily for DoS and USAID staff who have deployed to high-stress and high-threat environments. The High Stress Assignment Outbrief Program syllabus covers the following:

- Understanding the challenges of returning from a high-stress environment.
- Learning how to share information with your loved ones to ensure the kind of reunion you want and deserve.
- Identifying signs and symptoms of possible psychological reactions, including PTSD.
- Locating additional resources, if desired.
- Conveying to the State Department the full range of difficulties you encountered.[110]

DoS currently mandates that foreign service and civil service employees must attend the High Stress Assignment Outbrief Program if they have spent more than 90 days in the following countries:

January 19 and 31, 2017; RAND interviews with DoS officials, December 20, 2016, and January 23, 2017; RAND interviews with non-DoD federal officials, November 22, 2016, and January 13, 2017; RAND interview with non-DoD federal officials, November 21, 2016, and April 13, 2017; RAND interview with non-DoD federal official, March 15, 2017.

[110] DoS, undated-b.

Afghanistan, Iraq, Pakistan, Yemen, Libya, South Sudan, and the Central African Republic.[111] The FSI also encourages people to attend if they have been to other high-stress postings, and also allows people from agencies other than DoS to attend (at a tuition fee of $125). However, the interview sample for this study did not span individuals from non-DoS organizations who had attended or who knew that it was even an option. Notably, the FSI Transition Center also runs the Center of Excellence in Foreign Affairs Resilience, which offers and is continually developing training in resilience.

Individuals interviewed in several other agencies, such as the Department of Justice (specifically, DEA) and DHS, similarly had post-trauma practices, although none were as evolved as those offered by DoS. These practices were tailored to the specific agency and its mission, and they reflected the fact that personnel deployed by those agencies could be exposed to traumatic events. In situations where it was unlikely that staff would encounter traumatic events, the office or agency in question typically relied on its EAP to provide support. All agencies included in the interview sample reportedly had an EAP, and interviews indicated that EAPs seemed to be the default vehicle used to provide post-traumatic support if required. However, EAPs are not designed as post-deployment service providers and, therefore, are not optimized to help. Similarly, the range and quality of services can vary from program to program. Additionally, although managers interviewed noted EAPs as a mechanism for providing post-deployment care, employees from the same organizations were not always aware of the option.[112]

Civilians who suffer injury during a deployment receive critical care at military treatment facilities while deployed. However, upon return, care for injured civilian deployees is transferred administratively to the Department of Labor's OWCP under FECA authority (5 U.S.C. § 8101). Such benefits include medical care coverage, vocational rehabilitation, and death gratuities in the event the employee is killed in theater or later dies from injuries sustained during a deploy-

[111] DoS, undated-b.

[112] RAND interview with non-DoD federal employee, February 24, 2017.

ment.[113] Additionally, provisions within FECA ensure that, under certain "compelling circumstances," federal civilians injured during a deployment can request treatment at a military treatment facility if the nature of the injury requires specific treatment only available at such a facility.[114] However, DoD policy on the treatment of post-deployment civilians can be unclear, and non-DoD agencies are not always aware that their civilians might be eligible for treatment at military treatment facilities.

While deployed federal civilian employees do have access to FECA benefits, the burden of proof in the wake of an injury is much higher for deployed civilians than their uniformed counterparts. Civilians injured during deployment must provide detailed medical evidence to the OWCP. The OWCP acknowledges that "exigent circumstances attendant to deployment" may make it difficult for individuals to obtain the necessary medical evidence.[115] Federal civilians injured during a deployment often find the process cumbersome. One individual expressed frustration with the process in a September 2009 congressional hearing: "The military saves your life, gets you home, and then it's totally up to you."[116]

DoD experiences with post-trauma programs and activities for uniformed service members could potentially serve as a model for civilian agencies, but any potential program must be evaluated based on the evidentiary basis for its effectiveness and on its applicability to

---

[113] Office of Workers' Compensation Programs, Division of Federal Employees' Compensation (DFEC), "Information for Deployed Employees and Their Agencies Concerning the Federal Employees' Compensation Act," webpage, U.S. Department of Labor, undated.

[114] The Under Secretary of Defense for Personnel and Readiness is authorized to approve eligibility for non-DoD civilians who suffer injury or illness as the result of a deployment. For more information, see Deputy Secretary of Defense, "Policy Guidance for Provision of Medical Care to Department of Defense Civilian Employees Injured or Wounded While Forward Deployed in Support of Hostilities," memorandum to Department of Defense officials, Washington, D.C.: Office of the Secretary of Defense, September 24, 2007.

[115] "Issue Brief: Benefits for Deployed Civilians Vary," *FEDWeek*, August 26, 2009.

[116] Stephen F. Lynch, "A Call to Arms: A Review of Benefits for Deployed Federal Employees," testimony before the Subcommittee on Federal Workforce, Postal Service, and the District of Columbia, Committee on Oversight and Government Reform, U.S. House of Representatives, Washington, D.C., September 16, 2009.

and appropriateness for the particular civilian deployee population in question. However, several programs, such as the Army's Battlemind program and the OSCAR teams, have received positive independent evaluations. Therefore, they could be used as a starting point for federal agencies.

Personnel Tracking

The non-DoD federal agency offices included in the sample each had some form of management system that tracked personnel. During deployment, only two interviewees indicated they had contact with their parent organizations while deployed, even if they were being tracked by the organization to which they deployed.[117] However, once people returned, none of the departments interviewed had any formal means of tracking those who had deployed, beyond a note on their human resources records. Tracking personnel in the short term is important to ensure that people complete requisite reintegration or decompression programs and in the longer term to help build an awareness of who has deployed to a high-threat or high-stress environment and what impact that may have on them. The 2010 Office of Inspector General report identified this as an issue and recommended establishing a tracking system to ensure that people took the required post-deployment courses.[118]

The military services regularly track service members before, during, and after a deployment in multiple ways and archive those findings to improve their organizations over time. All military services have a large personnel office within their headquarters elements that are responsible for tracking service members and, although they do not centrally deploy personnel, they are able to quickly identify personnel who have deployed. Civilian agencies should consider having a central office to track both deployed personnel and those who have already returned from a deployment. Personnel tracking has numerous advan-

---

[117] RAND interviews with non-DoD federal officials, February 9, 2017, and March 16, 2017.

[118] U.S. Department of State, Broadcasting Board of Governors, Office of Inspector General, 2010, p. 1.

tages from a recruitment, training, experience, and a post-deployment health perspective. Organizations should track their deployees in an effort to track post-deployment health outcomes, as well as to more generally draw upon the deployment experiences of these individuals and to collect lessons learned to better prepare future deployees.

Workplace Reintegration

Because deployments are not a common experience for civilians across non-DoD federal agencies, some employees face challenges reintegrating in their workplaces. One interviewee noted that his or her workplace operates an internal labor market, and that he or she faced challenges finding assignments within the office upon his or her return.[119] A manager reported that their office found it necessary to create standard operating procedures protecting a deployed individual's office supplies (desks and chairs) and office space, because deployees who had lost their office space while deployed had, after returning from deployment, reported a sense that they no longer belonged in the office.[120]

---

[119] RAND interview with non-DoD federal employee, February 24, 2017.

[120] RAND interview with non-DoD federal official, February 21, 2017.

CHAPTER FOUR

Key Findings and Recommendations

Key Findings

Although this study has explored only a subset of the policies and programs in place for deploying civilians, several key issues associated with reintegrating civilian employees following a deployment emerged from the interviews. Moreover, the interview findings juxtaposed against the literature on successful practices in post-deployment reintegration of military personnel suggest the potential ways to ensure the availability of effective and equitable post-deployment reintegration practices for non-DoD federal civilian deployees.

More work remains to be done to comprehensively address this issue. However, this study suggests that policymakers and stakeholders consider the following nine key findings when taking further steps to develop and implement civilian post-deployment reintegration policies and practices.

Finding 1: Reliable Data to Document Needs and Measures of Effectiveness to Assess Program Utility Are Lacking

To date, no reliable data exist on the size and scale of the issues facing individual civilian deployees, and more evidence-based research is needed. Numerous studies have looked at pre-deployment resilience training practices within DoD and foreign defense organizations, including several evaluations of post-deployment reintegration policies and practices within DoD. However, little exists for the non-

DoD federal workforce. The various agencies that are the subject of this report collect very little data describing the scale and nature of the post-deployment issues that their redeployed civilian populations face. Meanwhile, very little implicit knowledge exists in the form of common operating procedures, lessons learned, or shared best practices for post-deployment reintegration across the interagency community. The only organization interviewed for this study that thinks in such collaborative, interagency terms regarding reintegration practices is the FSI, which provides several post-deployment classes and activities. Finally, measures of effectiveness (outcomes) to evaluate the effectiveness of reintegration programs are lacking at this point.

Overall, 12 of the 36 individuals interviewed for this study agreed that post-deployment reintegration was an important issue, but there was no agreement on what or how much should be done.[1] To fully understand the scope and scale of the issues facing these civilian agencies, additional research is needed; to facilitate such research, more-systematic data collection on this population and its needs and measures of effectiveness to assess program utility are required.

Finding 2: All Agencies Had a Pre-Deployment Process; Very Few Had a Formal Post-Deployment Process

There appears to be an imbalance in current non-DoD federal agency policy and practice with regard to civilian deployment: The majority of such organizations have carefully considered how best to prepare and deploy someone, and have established policies, procedures, and practices to do so. However, in many cases, leadership in these organizations have given little or no consideration to how best to reintegrate personnel after a deployment. Several of the agencies studied here are addressing this shortfall (e.g., the new initiatives by DEA), but many are not.

---

[1] RAND interviews with DEA officials, January 19 and 31, 2017; RAND interviews with DoS officials, January 12, 2017, and February 6, 2017; RAND interviews with FEMA officials, February 21 and 23, 2017, and March 6, 2017; RAND interview with SIGAR official, February 23, 2017; RAND interviews with USAID officials, November 22, 2016, and January 19, 2017.

All interviewees stated that they had gone through some form of pre-deployment process, although specific processes varied. However, none of the interviewees reported an employer requirement to proceed through any form of post-deployment or reintegration process. Although most deployees received some form of post-deployment leave, little occurred in the way of administrative processing, medical examinations, or debriefing, either in country or in the United States.[2] This was even true of individuals who had been deployed to high-risk countries and conflict areas.

DoS was the only non-DoD federal agency studied that mandated specific post-deployment activities, requiring that anyone deployed to a designated high-threat or high-stress mission undergo a mandatory out-briefing, and highly recommending this briefing for postings not meeting the "high-stress" or "high-risk" threshold. Although such a requirement is a solid first step toward establishment of effective reintegration practices, evidence from military post-deployment reintegration efforts—both in the United States and abroad—revealed multiple additional activities (some that are empirically supported and others that require additional research to assess their value) that non-DoD federal agencies might consider to better ensure effective reintegration of returned civilian deployees.

Finding 3: Civilian Post-Deployment Reintegration Concepts and Practices Vary Across U.S. Federal Agencies

Overall, this research found that there is a wide range in the provision of current civilian post-deployment reintegration concepts and practices across the federal government. Some organizations offer more expansive civilian post-deployment reintegration services than others. For example, the DEA and USAID appear to provide the most-comprehensive post-deployment reintegration processes. The DEA has modeled one of its programs on the U.S. military's YRRP, integrating a

---

2 RAND interview with Treasury official, February 24, 2017; RAND interview with DoC official, February 6, 2017; RAND interview with DEA official, January 31, 2017; RAND interview with DEA official, January 19, 2017; RAND interview with USCIS official, January 17, 2017; RAND interview with USAID official, November 22, 2016; RAND interview with OFDA official, March 15, 2017.

variety of reintegration, decompression, and post-trauma and resiliency practices into the program. For its part, USAID has developed Staff Care, which provides several reintegration activities for all USAID personnel (including local and national personnel). FSI, meanwhile, is a leader in developing resilience training and outbriefings for individuals returning from high-stress assignments.

Although DEA and USAID appear to provide fairly comprehensive post-deployment reintegration activities and programs for their civilian deployees, the research team found little evidence of any common concept of post-deployment reintegration or standards of best practice for civilian reintegration across the interagency community. Ultimately, many agencies use either no or minimal post-deployment reintegration practices; with few exceptions, those that do exist tend to consist largely of administrative procedures. Most agencies follow DoS guidelines for their pre-deployment, in-country, and post-deployment practices.

Finding 4: Administrative Outprocessing and Post-Deployment Leave Appear to Be the Only Post-Deployment Reintegration Practices Consistently Offered to Civilian Deployees

As noted above, interviewees from six offices indicated that their respective organizations provide some form of post-deployment leave, even if they had no other form of post-deployment policy or practice.[3] This was one of only two consistent post-deployment activities that were identified during the course of this research; the second was administrative outprocessing. Although it was outside the scope of this research to test hypotheses as to why these two activities are the most prevalent among federal agencies, this would be a fruitful avenue for future research. It is possible that these activities are viewed by the leadership of the organizations in question to be less costly than other reintegration activities, and/or to benefit multiple organizational objectives

[3] RAND interview with non-DoD federal official, March 14, 2017; RAND interviews with non-DoD federal officials, December 29, 2016, and January 12, 2017; RAND interview with non-DoD official, March 17, 2017; RAND interview with OIE official, February 15, 2017; RAND interview with SIGAR official, February 23, 2017; RAND interviews with Treasury officials, February 9 and 24, 2017, and March 16, 2017.

simultaneously. Nevertheless, the role of post-deployment leave in post-deployment reintegration is unknown and an important area of study.

Finding 5: Individual Versus Unit Deployments Affect Reintegration Processes Differently

U.S. civilian and DoD organizations differ significantly in a manner affecting their employees' respective post-deployment reintegration experiences—specifically, the services frequently deploy military personnel in units, and civilian agencies almost exclusively deploy personnel as individuals. Although there are instances in which the military will deploy individual augmentees to a variety of headquarters and operational units, and there are several policies and practices that govern both individual and unit deployments, the military often deploys personnel in units.[4]

For planning purposes, the U.S. Army traditionally thinks of capabilities in terms of personnel units or equipment packages, Air Force planners think in terms of air frames, and Navy planners think in terms of ship-borne capabilities. Deployment within a unit structure matters, because it means that personnel then go through a deployment and the ensuing redeployment process with their peers and as a group. Reintegration processes can be tailored to a returning unit's schedule and organized such that returned deployees are presented with relevant reintegration information in a group format in a timely fashion.

Meanwhile, non-DoD federal agency personnel—who primarily deploy as individuals—proceed through the reintegration processes individually (or, in many cases, not at all). As a result, agency reintegration processes tend to operate in a more piecemeal fashion, if at all, which translates into little standardization of post-deployment reintegration practices across the interagency community. Therefore, individuals deployees are more likely to fall through the cracks upon redeployment than are individuals who deploy as a unit and have established programs for reintegration when they return.

---

[4] Even for personnel that deploy individually, there are locations which routinely deploy service members. These locations have well established policies and procedures that govern the deployment process.

Finding 6: One's Employment Category Affects His or Her Reintegration Options

A civilian's employment category appears to affect his or her post-deployment reintegration options. As discussed in further detail below, the provision of current civilian post-deployment reintegration concepts and practices varies widely across the federal government, with many depending upon the type of authority under which an individual is hired. In addition to the three employment categories previously described (e.g., civil service, foreign service, and PSCs), there are several other non-DoD civilian employment categories, including reservists,[5] intermittent staff, government service employees, and local national personnel. Relevant categories of civilian deployment across DoD include civil service, PSCs, and intermittent staff.

Employment categories are significant because deployment systems, processes, and support, as well as post-deployment reintegration practices, were all designed first and foremost for foreign service cadres rather than civil servants. As a greater number and broader range of U.S. government civilian employees deploy, modification of current deployment and post-deployment processes are necessary. The increased number of U.S. civil servants deploying to high-threat or high-stress environments only heightens the need for such processes to be modified to fit their deployments.

Moreover, as discussed in greater detail in the next finding, PSCs—because of the temporary nature of their affiliation with a particular agency—often fall outside the scope of the few post-deployment reintegration practices and programs that do exist for non-DoD federal civilians.

Finding 7: Personal Services Contractors Typically Receive No Post-Deployment Reintegration Support

PSCs are more difficult to track following the end of their contract—which sometimes aligns with the culmination of a deployment, but at other times occurs at a pre-specified end-date, such as two years from

---

[5] Note that the term *reservist* here refers to non-DoD federal agency reservists, who deploy in civilian status. U.S. military reserve component members are not within the study's scope, because they deploy in uniformed status.

the signing of the contract. Therefore, they may not be screened or provided with adequate services for post-deployment health issues, among other reintegration challenges.[6] Although the level of post-deployment support varied among regular government employees, several of those interviewed had been PSCs during their careers. None of those current or former PSCs interviewed had received any form of post-deployment support, and the research team was unable to find any examples of PSCs who had received post-deployment support.[7]

The question this raises is whether PSCs represent a hidden community with unseen issues within the wider community of deployed civilians. The USAID report on stress also identified this issue, stating that, at least within the USAID context, "PSCs are deeply and particularly affected by the failures of the human resources management function and administrative support systems to meet their somewhat unique situations and needs."[8] Given that PSCs form a pool from which future deployees are drawn, this could present issues for future missions and deployments.[9]

Finding 8: Civilian Deployees Must Actively Seek Assistance, But Lack Knowledge Regarding Availability of Post-Deployment Reintegration Activities

The single biggest obstacle to accessing post-deployment services (i.e., administrative, medical, or otherwise) was that people had to ask for help. Numerous interviewees reported that deployees are required to actively seek out desired reintegration assistance. Yet, during the course of the 36 interviews, it became apparent that many personnel were unsure of either the policies or practices that govern the post-deployment process for their own agency. Even in cases in which returned deployees were willing to ask for help, interviews revealed that they did not know of the various

---

6 Marcia Carruthers and Carol A. Harnett, *Workplace Warriors: The Corporate Response to Deployment and Reintegration*, Hartford, Conn.: The Hartford Group, 2008, p. 6.

7 RAND interview with DoC official, February 6, 2017; RAND interview with USAID official, November 22, 2016.

8 Greenleaf Integrative Strategies, 2015, p. 51.

9 For more on rules and regulations concerning PSCs, see U.S. Department of State, "Personal Services Contractors (PSC)," *Foreign Affairs Manual*, Vol. 3, Chapter 9000, 2017a.

available services, and so they were unaware of what to request in terms of assistance and services.

Adding to the confusion was a lack of mutual understanding between deployed and home organizations. Whereas some organizations kept in touch with their personnel when deployed, others did not maintain regular communication. This lack of communication led to misperceptions and unmet expectations when personnel redeployed to their home organizations. For example, one non-DoD interviewee noted the tensions generated when a deployed civilian's portfolios or physical office space were reassigned during deployment, stating, "When you deploy, it doesn't mean you got a new job."[10] Another factor adding to the confusion was that most agencies deployed their personnel out of their own office and did not maintain centralized deployment offices knowledgeable in all facets of deployment and redeployment.

To the extent that well-defined policy forms a basis for effective practice, this speaks to a need for the respective non-DoD federal agencies deploying civilians to define and specify their own individual guidance regarding post-deployment reintegration as a first step to ensuring improved and systematized reintegration programs, activities, and overall practice.

Finding 9: Seeking Assistance Is Stigmatized in Some Cases

Some interviewees expressed concerns about asking for help. They were concerned about any stigma that might be associated with asking for assistance and what impact this might have on them or their careers in the short or long term.[11] Both the 2010 report and the 2015 USAID report on stress identified the issue of stigma in seeking help, especially with regard to psychological issues.[12]

[10] Interview with non-DoD agency official, February 21, 2019.

[11] RAND interview with SIGAR official, February 23, 2017; RAND interview with DoS official, January 23, 2017; RAND interview with USAID official, January 13, 2017; RAND interview with USAID official, November 22, 2016.

[12] DoS, Broadcasting Board of Governors, Office of Inspector General, 2010, p. 1; Greenleaf Integrative Strategies, 2015, p. 100.

Recommendations

In light of the these findings, the research team recommends that U.S. federal agencies take the following actions to help ensure the health and welfare of their civilian agency workforces through successful post-deployment reintegration activities, practices, and programs.

Individual Agencies Should Mandate Exit Interviews During the Redeployment Process

To assist organizations in tracking their deployees and gain useful feedback on deployment-related issues, all deployees should go through a mandatory exit interview. This interview could be with home organization management and could be used to summarize what went well and what did not during the deployment. This process could help future deployees understand the issues of deployment and be better prepared to confront them. It could also be used to collect best practices for the organization and could help to identify future policies and practices.

Individual Agencies Should Establish Processes to Effectively Track Civilians, Including Personal Services Contractors, Following a Deployment

The ability to account for civilian personnel while deployed typically falls under the Chief of Mission of the embassy or military command where the civilian in question is deployed. After deployees return from a deployment, civilian agencies should consider continuing to monitor and account for these individuals in their workforce. The ability to track returned personnel provides several benefits; it allows for easy medical follow-up at pre-identified critical times for redeployed personnel, and it offers the ability to quickly provide a snapshot of deployed personnel in the workforce, the time they spent deployed, and how long ago they returned from a deployment. In some cases where large numbers of PSCs are deployed, this may be logistically challenging; in others, where relatively few PSCs deploy (and deploy repeatedly), this may be more feasible and potentially useful.

Individual Agencies Deploying Civilians Should Raise Awareness of Existing Policies, Programs, and Activities—And, in Doing So, Destigmatize Efforts to Seek Help

Agencies should prioritize efforts to raise awareness among civilian employees of the post-deployment reintegration policies, programs, and activities that are already in place within their organizations. Although the policies and practices vary across organization, all organizations have at least some practices in place to deal with post-deployment reintegration. The establishment of comprehensive policy for the post-deployment reintegration process could help to ensure employees understand the process and what resources are available to them, and to improve reintegration overall.

For example, every agency included in the interview sample had some type of administrative process in place. Administrative activities varied by organization, but most were not comprehensive and did not supply a simple checklist of administrative activities that needed to be complete upon redeployment. Building a comprehensive, step-by-step checklist—to help ensure that deployees understand the redeployment process and relevant points of contact upon redeployment—would help to alleviate strain and make the redeployment process smoother.

In messaging the availability of post-deployment reintegration programs and activities to deployed civilian populations, agencies should place special emphasis on destigmatizing access to these programs. This is true for all programs, but particularly important in the case of those aimed at improving mental health outcomes.

Both DoD and Non-DoD Federal Agencies Should Work Together to Consolidate and Centralize Civilian Post-Deployment Reintegration Activities, Practices, and Programs

The non-DoD federal agency community should consider increased centralization of operational responsibilities for civilian post-deployment reintegration between agencies. This has strong potential to both reduce transaction costs and identify best practices amongst a variety of reintegration alternatives. Although several consolidated training centers for deploying personnel currently exist, such as FSI, the Indiana National Guard's Camp Atterbury, and the Defense Intelligence Agency's Expeditionary Readiness Center, there is no equivalent for returning civilian personnel. Indeed, several interviewees noted the lack of a centralized process upon their redeployment and how each individual experienced something different.[13] One individual noted that this led to a "very disorganized"[14] process, and others commented on how a more formal process would be helpful.[15] As noted in one interview, "We don't have any resources devoted to any sort of formal program on reintegration back into headquarters. I would love to be able to have something like that. EAPs aren't currently designed to be helpful to people returning from overseas."[16]

FSI could continue to be used as a center for training and education for returned civilian deployees across the interagency community. The recently created "resiliency center" adds to the suite of capabilities that the DoS can offer, but post-deployment stress management training is still limited in scope and scale. USAID's Staff Care could also be used as a potential source to provides services for returning civilian personnel across the interagency, though it would have to be resourced adequately from pooled funds across the interagency community to do so.

Finally, it may make sense for DoD and non-DoD federal agencies to coordinate on the timing of sending their respective deployees through a reintegration program. Although it would be ideal for such reintegration to take place immediately after returning, DoD and service experiences with military reintegration programs indicate that the ability to send entire units through a reintegration program simultaneously could be valuable in terms of allowing for the program to be appropriately scaled (i.e., sufficient resources can be devoted to it and it can be aimed at a large-enough population that it can be structured in a valuable way) and to provide a peer network of fellow returned

---

[13] RAND interview with Treasury official, February 9, 2017; RAND interview with USCIS official, January 17, 2017; RAND interview with FEMA official, March 6 , 2017.

[14] RAND interview with Treasury official, February 9, 2017.

[15] RAND interview with FEMA official, March 6, 2017; RAND interview with DoC official, February 6, 2017.

[16] RAND interview with Treasury official, February 9, 2017.

deployees. Therefore, because U.S. federal civilians typically do not deploy in units, coordination among agencies to mimic the unit construct by aggregating individual deployees across agencies into groups and sending them through post-deployment reintegration programs together could be beneficial in multiple ways. Attempts to mimic unit constructs may be somewhat limited by distinctions between deploying civilians' employment categories; for example, it may be more challenging to compel a PSC returning from a deployment to pass through a reintegration program at the end of his or her deployment and contract term than it would be to mandate that a civil servant or foreign service officer do the same. However, such challenges could be fairly easily surmounted through the modification of contract language in personal services contracts to mandate reintegration program participation and the extension of contract terms to allow for such participation.

Federal Agencies Should Consider Implementation of Numerous Military Reintegration Solutions, Adapted for Their Deployed Civilian Populations

Promising military post-deployment reintegration practices relevant to the non-DoD federal civilian population exist. As noted in Chapter Two, Battlemind is an Army program with a post-deployment component that could be adopted to different settings. OSCAR is a Marine Corps–developed program that uses a multidisciplinary team of health care providers, family, and religious personnel that help marines with combat stress problems. Each of these programs use operational debriefing and stress debriefing, which have at least some proven benefits.

Elements of these programs could be used as a model and adapted by non-DoD agencies for their deployed civilian personnel. Specifically, where civilian personnel are deployed to high-stress environments, a more comprehensive program—such as Battlemind or OSCAR, or something similar tailored to agency needs—should be considered to provide the necessary access to reintegration activities and programs following a deployment. Other military post-deployment reintegration practices may also be usefully adapted to the civilian sphere, although the needs and characteristics of the particular agency and civilian population in question will need to be considered carefully to find alignment with a potentially comparable military practice.

Individual Agencies and Both DoD and Non-DoD Federal Agency Communities Should Conduct Further Evidence-Based Research on Civilian Deployees and Post-Deployment Reintegration Activities

This report builds on an existing, small body of research that examines post-deployment reintegration efforts by several U.S. agencies. However, for the most part, evidence and systematic evaluations of U.S. federal civilian deployment experiences—and particularly the post-deployment stage—have been lacking, and there has been no substantial examination into the various categories of personnel eligible for particular activities. More research is needed to explore which activities, practices, and programs are most effective at returning civilians to their home offices following a deployment. Specific potential areas for further exploration include

- differences between military and civilian deployees (e.g., demographic characteristics, unit versus individual deployment, functions performed, likelihood of multiple deployments) and the effects of those differences on (1) the deployees' needs for reintegration services and (2) the agencies' incentives to provide reintegration services
- differences among civilian deployees (e.g., demographic characteristics, employment category, functions performed, likelihood of multiple deployments) across the federal agencies, including DoD, and the effects of those differences on (1) the deployees' needs for reintegration services and (2) the agencies' incentives to provide reintegration services
- evaluations of current civilian reintegration programs
- selection of military reintegration programs for adaptation to the civilian population
- piloting new civilian reintegration programs, including a formal evaluation
- exploration of agencies' incentives for providing civilian reintegration programs, particularly related to incentives to maintain an

adequate, satisfied labor pool willing to undertake multiple civilian deployments.

This research should measure both the effectiveness of the respective activities and programs and the associated cost. Although some military reintegration programs have been subject to rigorous, refereed evaluation, there are virtually no analogous studies that exist for the civilian workforce.

Conclusion

The primary goal of this research, as elaborated in Chapter One, was to identify policy and practices used by U.S. non-DoD federal agencies to understand the specific policies, processes, tools, and outputs associated with civilian post-deployment reintegration. To do this, the research team: (1) used the U.S. military case to explore current post-deployment reintegration policies and practices for U.S. service members, highlighting key categories of activities and promising practices for potential adaptation to the civilian sphere; (2) identified and explored existing U.S. federal agency policies and practices for civilian post-deployment reintegration, and (3) made policy recommendations to ensure that civilians receive adequate and appropriate support when returning from a deployment.

Overall, we found little evidence to show that the U.S. federal civilian agencies examined in this research have been systematically thinking about post-deployment reintegration in any type of methodical fashion. Although some agencies have devoted resources to the issue, most agencies have little in the way of either (1) an overarching philosophy or conceptualization of post-deployment reintegration; (2) established policy regarding reintegration; or (3) actual reintegration programs in place for their returning deployees. Significant knowledge and capability gaps exist both within and across the various agencies. Additionally, there has been little in the way of research into post-deployment reintegration activities that might potentially be applicable to and effective within the context of U.S. federal agencies.

Although this report explores potential avenues for modeling federal civilian reintegration programs on existing military reintegration programs, the topic poses fruitful ground for further in-depth study on alignment of particular programs with specific civilian populations.

The findings presented in this report should be of interest to a wide variety of policymakers, managers, and personnel in federal agencies that routinely deploy personnel domestically or internationally to high-threat or high-stress environments. Moreover, from a personnel-management standpoint, this research is intended to inform researchers and decisionmakers who are interested in developing methods and strategies to more effectively and efficiently reintegrate civilians following a deployment.

APPENDIX A

Glossary of Relevant Terms

Administrative outprocessing: Tasks that must be completed upon returning from deployment—for example, turning in equipment, badges and passports, updating health care forms, and various debriefings. These tasks are often accomplished with the use of checklists and are generally completed upon return to the home office, although a portion of the tasks can be completed at the deployment location.[1]

Community and family reintegration: Consists of several different categories:

- **Transition from the deployed experience back to the home organization:** Activities might include a return-to-work planning meeting with management, a "welcome home" meeting with management and/or "sharing the story" talk or presentation.
- **Family activities:** Briefings workshops or events where spouses, children, or both attend with the deployee. Activities could include budgeting and financial management, reintegrating with children and spouses, stress management, sleep counseling, nutrition, and well-being.

Decompression program: Process designed to help personnel returning from deployment to and to promote a positive psychological

[1] U.S. Department of the Navy, *Redeployment and Demobilization Administrative Screening Checklist*, NAVPERS 1300/23, August 2012.

response to deployment trauma.[2] Common elements include rest and recuperation and debriefing. Decompression often takes place in a third location, neither home nor theater, so deployees can adjust without the stresses of the combat zone or civilian life.[3]

Employee assistance programs: EAP is defined by OPM as a "voluntary, work-based program that offers free and confidential assessments, short-term counseling, referrals, and follow-up services to employees who have personal and/or work-related problems."[4]

Deployment: The movement of personnel to a place or position for a specific action and time period.[5] For the purposes of this study, we considered both overseas and domestic deployments to a theater of conflict or disaster area.[6]

Health assessments: Consists of both DoD and civilian agency processes. DoD uses the Post-Deployment Health Assessment form (DD Form 2796),[7] the Post-Deployment Health Reassessment form (DD Form 2900),[8] and the Deployment Mental Health Assessment form (DD Form 2978)[9] to ascertain a deployee's mental and medical condition. Deployed personnel must complete the assessments according to a specific time frame. Following completion of the forms,

---

2 Hacker Hughes et al., 2008, p. 534.

3 Schell et al., 2016, p. ix.

4 U.S. Office of Personnel Management, undated-b.

5 The Cambridge Dictionary defines *deployment* as "the movement of soldiers or equipment to a place where they can be used when they are needed." We expanded this definition to include specific actions for a specific time period to encompass civilian personnel movements in support of agency missions. See Cambridge Dictionary, "Deployment," webpage, undated.

6 Other terms relevant to this research are defined in this glossary.

7 U.S. Department of Defense, 2015a.

8 U.S. Department of Defense, 2015b.

9 U.S. Department of Defense, "Deployment Mental Health Assessment," DD Form 2978, February 2014.

a health care provider reviews the form and conducts a face-to-face interview.[10]

Personnel tracking: The tracking of personnel during and after a deployment. The military tracks the personnel tempo (PERSTEMPO) events of all service members, in which a transaction record is submitted every time an event (such as an operation, exercise, or training) begins and ends.[11]

Post-deployment leave: There are three categories of post-deployment leave:

- **Decompression leave**: Also known as Special Leave Accrual, which is specific to DoD and grants additional leave, above the normal limits, for deployees assigned to hostile fire or imminent danger areas.[12]
- **Administrative absence**: Absence, not credited as leave, authorized for specific reasons, such as attending professional meetings, board meetings and seminars, house-hunting, a post-deployment or mobilization respite absence, and a transition leave of absence.[13]
- **Normal accrued leave**: Accrued or accumulated annual or sick leave.[14] Within DoD, leave is accrued at a rate of 2.5 days per month of active service and credited to the service member's leave account.[15] Leave for civilians is based on a number of employment

---

[10] Psychological Health Center of Excellence, "Deployment Health Assessments," webpage, undated.

[11] DoDI 1336.07, *Reporting of Personnel Tempo (PERSTEMPO) Events*, Washington, D.C.: U.S. Department of Defense, July 28, 2009, p. 12.

[12] DoDI 1327.06, *Leave and Liberty Policy and Procedures*, Washington, D.C.: U.S. Department of Defense, May 19, 2016, p. 8.

[13] DoDI 1327.06, 2016, pp. 25–26.

[14] DoS, "Shared Voluntary Leave Programs," *Foreign Affairs Manual*, Vol. 3, Chapter 3340, October 2019c; DoS, "Definitions," *Foreign Affairs Manual*, Vol. 3, Chapter 3342, July 28, 2015.

[15] DoDI 1327.06, 2016, p. 46.

categories. Full-time employees generate from one half day (four hours) up to one day (eight hours) for each pay period, depending on length of service.[16]

Post-deployment reintegration: The resumption of age, gender, and culturally appropriate roles in the family, community, and workplace and the process of transitioning back into personal and organizational roles following deployment.[17] Composed of activities, programs, and practices designed to provide support to service members and civilians upon return from a deployment. Post-deployment reintegration *activities* entail a specific event or function. Post-deployment reintegration *programs* comprise specific activities organized around a general theme or subset of reintegration (e.g., family reintegration). Post-deployment reintegration *practices* encompass both activities and programs.

Post-trauma practices: Practices intended to help deployees with the psychological aftermath of a stressful or traumatic incident. Examples include crisis incident stress management, peer-to-peer counseling, and mentorship.

Recognition: Decorations, awards, and events for service members and civilians after return from a deployment.[18]

Redeployment: The return of personnel, equipment, and materiel to the home and/or demobilization stations for reintegration and/or outprocessing.[19]

---

[16] Civilians accrue leave in accordance with OPM policy. See U.S. Office of Personnel Management, "Pay & Leave: Leave Administration," webpage, undated-c.

[17] Shannon L. Currie, Arla Day, and E. Kevin Kelloway, "Bringing the Troops Back Home: Modeling the Post Deployment Reintegration Experience," *Journal of Occupational Health Psychology*, Vol. 16, No. 1, January 2011.

[18] DoDI 1348.33, 2016.

[19] Joint Publication 1-02, *Dictionary of Associated Military Terms*, Washington, D.C.: U.S. Joint Chiefs of Staff, November 8, 2010, as amended through February 15, 2016.

Resilience training: Training designed to improve performance in combat and prevent mental health problems, including depression, PTSD, and suicide.[20] Based on practices from positive psychology, resiliency training is focused not on treatment, but on prevention, and enhancement.

---

[20] Benedict Carey, "Mental Health Training is Planned for U.S. Soldiers," *New York Times*, August 17, 2009.

APPENDIX B

Interview Protocol

Type of Personnel

- Are you a deploying official or do you deploy yourself?

Organizational Background Questions

- For what purposes are civilians deployed from your organization?
- How large is your organization's potential deployable civilian force? Is it composed of full-time employees, temporary employees, contractors (i.e., under what hiring mechanisms are deployable civilians hired)?

Redeployment Process

- Can you please walk me through a typical redeployment? What are individuals required to do? What programs are offered? Is there a formal checklist delineating this process? Can you recommend potential interviewees who oversee this process?

- Do individuals go through any formal or required programs upon redeployment?
  - Do individuals have mandatory programs or activities to complete?
  - Is there a formal "welcome home" event?
  - Are deployees recognized formally? Medal? Award? Bonus?
- Does the redeployment process differ for full-time employees? Contractors? Temporary employees?
- Does your organization use any third location decompression sites?
- Do any voluntary reintegration programs exist? What are they?
  - For example, are there any informal networks or groups, listservs that personnel can join to talk about their deployments?
- Are you encouraged to take leave following a deployment? If so, for how long?
- Do civilians complete a Post-Deployment Health Assessment (PDHA)? What does that look like, and who administers/assesses it?
- If post-deployment health care is accessed through your agency following a deployment, through what organization is this typically accessed? What is the statute of limitations for care (i.e., how long is care provided following a deployment)?

Organizational Policy

- What are the goals of your organization's policies for post-deployment reintegration?
  - Are your organization's policies designed to provide

  - emergency and casualty care?
  - promote long-term physical and mental fitness?
  - maintain readiness for future deployments in your organization?
- Is there a program office within your organization devoted entirely to the deployment and re-deployment of civilians? If not, how is it handled?

- Does a policy exist to separate personnel from the organization in the event that they can no longer perform their duties upon redeployment?

Human Resources—Personnel Actions

- Are deployed civilians tracked upon return? If so, how, and for what purpose (e.g., tracking, follow-up care)?

- Does your organization maintain an administrative checklist of tasks to complete prior to or upon redeployment?

- Does your organization have an Employee Assistance Program?

In Conclusion

- What are the barriers and facilitators to successful post-deployment reintegration policy and programs?

- What should be done to improve civilian post-deployment reintegration?

Bibliography

Adler, Amy B., Paul D. Bliese, Dennis McGurk, Charles W. Hoge, and Carl Andrew Castro, "Battlemind Debriefing and Battlemind Training as Early Interventions with Soldiers Returning From Iraq: Randomization by Platoon," *Journal of Consulting and Clinical Psychology,* Vol. 77, No. 5, October 2009, pp. 928–940.

Adler, Amy B., Brett T. Litz, Carl Andrew Castro, Michael Suvak, Jeffrey L. Thomas, Lolita Burrell, Dennis McGurk, Kathleen M. Wright, and Paul D. Bliese, "Group Randomized Trial of Critical Incident Stress Debriefing Provided to U.S. Peacekeepers," *Journal of Traumatic Stress*, Vol. 21, No. 3, June 2008, pp. 253–263.

Adler, Amy B., Carl Andrew Castro, and Dennis McGurk, "Time-Driven Battlemind Psychological Debriefing: A Group-Level Early Intervention in Combat," *Military Medicine*, Vol. 1, No. 21, January 2009, pp. 21–28.

AFI—*See* Air Force Instruction.

Allen, David G., Phillip C. Bryant, and James M. Vardaman. "Retaining Talent: Replacing Misconceptions With Evidence-Based Strategies," *Academy of Management Perspectives*, Vol. 24, No. 2, May 2010, pp. 48–64.

Army Public Health Center, "Combat Stress Control," U.S. Department of the Army, webpage, last updated December 15, 2017. As of October 28, 2019: https://phc.amedd.army.mil/topics/healthyliving/bh/Pages/CombatOperationalStressControl.aspx

Assistant Secretary of Defense, "Policy for Use of Force Protection Prescription Products," memorandum to Department of Defense officials, Washington, D.C., April 24, 2003.

Barnett, Lerner, Karsen, Frankel, and Castro Professional Association, "Support Tools for Civilian Contractors Returning from Overseas," webpage, undated. As of October 28, 2019:
http://injuredoverseas.com/support-tools-for-civilian-contractors-returning-from-overseas/#respond

Beckner, Christian, "A Quiet But Notable Reorganization at DHS Headquarters," *Security Insights*, webpage, February 3, 2015. As of December 12, 2019: https://www.securityinsights.org/2015/02/a-quiet-but-notable-reorganization-at-dhs-headquarters/.

Berry, John, "Deployed Federal Civilians: Advancing Security and Opportunity in Afghanistan," statement before the Subcommittee on Oversight of Government Management, the Federal Workforce, and the District of Columbia Committee on Homeland Security and Governmental Affairs, U.S. Senate, Washington, D.C., April 14, 2010.

Bierman, Alex, and Ryan Kelty, "The Threat of War and Psychological Distress Among Civilians Working in Iraq and Afghanistan," *Social Psychology Quarterly*, Vol. 77, No. 1, 2014, pp. 27–53.

Booz Allen Hamilton, *2014 Quadrennial Fire Review: Final Report*, Washington, D.C.: U.S. Department of Agriculture Forest Service Fire and Aviation Management, and Department of the Interior Office of Wildland Fire, May 2015. As of October 28, 2019: https://www.forestsandrangelands.gov/documents/qfr/2014QFRFinalReport.pdf

Brown, James C., "Warrior Transition Program Expands," U.S. Navy, Expeditionary Combat Readiness Center Public Affairs, February 9, 2017. As of October 28, 2019: http://www.navy.mil/submit/display.asp?story_id=98810

Cambridge Dictionary, "Deployment," webpage, undated. As of August 14, 2018: http://dictionary.cambridge.org/us/dictionary/english/deployment

Carey, Benedict, "Mental Health Training Is Planned for U.S. Soldiers," *New York Times*, August 17, 2009.

Carruthers, Marcia, and Carol A. Harnett, *Workplace Warriors: The Corporate Response to Deployment and Reintegration*, Hartford, Conn.: The Hartford Group, 2008.

Casey, George W., Jr., "Comprehensive Soldier Fitness: A Vision for Psychological Resilience in the U.S. Army," *American Psychologist*, Vol. 66, No. 1, January 2011, pp. 1–3.

Castro, Carl Andrew, "The U.S. Framework for Understanding, Preventing, and Caring for the Mental Health Needs of Service Members Who Served in Combat in Afghanistan and Iraq: A Brief Review of the Issues and the Research," *European Journal of Psychotraumatology*, Vol. 5, 2014.

Castro, Carl Andrew, Amy B. Adler, Dennis McGurk, and Paul D. Bliese. "Mental Health Training With Soldiers Four Months After Returning From Iraq: Randomization by Platoon," *Journal of Traumatic Stress*, Vol. 25, No. 4, August 2012, pp. 376–383

Code of Federal Regulations, Title 38, Pensions, Bonuses, and Veterans' Relief, Chapter 1, Section 21.9700, Yellow Ribbon G.I. Education Enhancement Program. As of December 12, 2019:
https://www.govinfo.gov/content/pkg/CFR-2011-title38-vol2/pdf/CFR-2011-title38-vol2-sec21-9700.pdf

Committee on the Assessment of Readjustment Needs of Military Personnel, Veterans, and Their Families, Board on the Health of Select Populations, and the Institute of Medicine, *Returning Home from Iraq and Afghanistan: Assessment of Readjustment Systematic Review of Interventions in Non-Clinical Samples of Adults*, Washington, D.C.: National Academies Press, March 12, 2013.

Cornell University, Department of Human Ecology, Family Life Development Center, *U.S. Army Deployment Readiness Handbook for DA Civilians and Family Members*, United States Army, Family and Morale, Welfare and Recreation Command, 2010.

Cornum, Rhonda, Michael D. Matthews, and Martin E.P. Seligman, "Comprehensive Solider Fitness: Building Resilience in a Challenging Institutional Context," *American Psychologist*, Vol. 66, No. 1, January 2011, pp. 4–9.

Currie, Shannon L., Arla Day, and E. Kevin Kelloway, "Bringing the Troops Back Home: Modeling the Post Deployment Reintegration Experience," *Journal of Occupational Health Psychology*, Vol. 16, No. 1, January 2011, pp. 38–47.

Deaton, Bob, "CISM Guidelines for Fire Management," National Interagency Fire Center, June 2010.

DeBruyne, Nese F., *American War and Military Operations Casualties: Lists and Statistics*, Washington, D.C.: Congressional Research Service, September 24, 2019. As of December 12, 2019:
https://fas.org/sgp/crs/natsec/RL32492.pdf

Department of Defense Directive 1404.10, *DoD Civilian Expeditionary Workforce,* Washington, D.C.: U.S. Department of Defense, January 23, 2009.

Department of Defense Directive 1400.31, *DoD Civilian Work Force Contingency and Emergency Planning and Execution,* Washington, D.C.: U.S. Department of Defense, April 28, 1995.

Department of Defense Directive 3000.05, *Military Support for Stability, Security, Transition, and Reconstruction (SSTR) Operations*, Washington, D.C.: U.S. Department of Defense, November 28, 2005.

Department of Defense Directive 6490.02E, *Comprehensive Health Surveillance*, Washington, D.C.: U.S. Department of Defense, October 3, 2013.

Department of Defense Instruction 1235.11, *Management of Individual Mobilization Augmentees (IMAs)*, Washington, D.C.: U.S. Department of Defense, July 10, 2015.

Department of Defense Instruction 1300.18, *Department of Defense (DoD) Personnel Casualty Matters, Policies, and Procedures*, Washington, D.C.: U.S. Department of Defense, August 14, 2009.

Department of Defense Instruction 1327.06, *Leave and Liberty Policy and Procedures*, Washington, D.C.: U.S. Department of Defense, May 19, 2016.

Department of Defense Instruction 1336.5, *Automated Extract of Active Duty Military Personnel Records*, Washington, D.C.: U.S. Department of Defense, May 2, 2001.

Department of Defense Instruction 1336.07, *Reporting of Personnel Tempo (PERSTEMPO) Events*, Washington, D.C.: U.S. Department of Defense, July 28, 2009.

Department of Defense Instruction 1342.28, *DoD Yellow Ribbon Reintegration Program (YRRP)*, Washington, D.C.: U.S. Department of Defense, March 20, 2011.

Department of Defense Instruction 1348.33, *DoD Military Awards and Recognition Program*, Washington, D.C.: U.S. Department of Defense, December 21, 2016.

Department of Defense Instruction 1400.32, *DoD Civilian Work Force Contingency and Emergency Planning Guidelines and Procedures*, U.S. Department of Defense, 1995.

Department of Defense Instruction 3002.03, *DoD Personnel Recovery–Reintegration of Recovered Personnel*, incorporating change 1, Washington, D.C.: U.S. Department of Defense, April 26, 2016.

Department of Defense Instruction 6200.06, *Periodic Health Assessment (PHA) Program*, Washington, D.C.: U.S. Department of Defense, September 8, 2016.

Department of Defense Instruction 6490.03, *Deployment Health*, Washington, D.C.: U.S. Department of Defense, June 19, 2019.

Department of Defense Instruction 6490.05, *Maintenance of Psychological Health in Military Operations*, Washington, D.C.: U.S. Department of Defense, October 2, 2013.

Department of Defense Instruction 6490.12, *Mental Health Assessments for Service Members Deployed in Connection with a Contingency Operation*, Washington, D.C.: U.S. Department of Defense, February 26, 2013.

Department of Defense Manual 1348.33, *Manual of Military Decorations and Awards: DoD Service Awards—Campaign, Expeditionary, and Service Medals*, Vol. 2, Washington, D.C.: U.S. Department of Defense, December 21, 2016a.

Department of Defense Manual 1348.33, *Manual of Military Decorations and Awards: DoD Service Awards: DoD-Wide Personal Performance and Valor Decorations*, Vol. 3, Washington, D.C.: U.S. Department of Defense, December 21, 2016b.

Deputy Secretary of Defense, "Policy Guidance for Provision of Medical Care to Department of Defense Civilian Employees Injured or Wounded While Forward Deployed in Support of Hostilities," memorandum to Department of Defense officials, Washington, D.C.: Office of the Secretary of Defense, September 24, 2007.

Deputy Secretary of Defense, "Supporting Civilian Personnel Requirements in Afghanistan," memorandum to Department of Defense officials, Washington, D.C., September 8, 2016.

De Soir, Erik, *The Belgian End of Mission Transition Period: Lessons Learned from Third Location Decompression After Operational Deployment*, Brussels, Belgium: North Atlantic Treaty Organization, RTO-MP-HFM-205, April 2011.

De Soir, Erik, "Psychological Adjustment After Military Operations: The Utility of Postdeployment Decompression for Supporting Health Readjustment," in Stephen V. Bowles and Paul T. Bartone, eds., *Handbook of Military Psychology: Clinical and Organizational Practice*, Cham, Switzerland: Springer, 2017, pp. 89–103.

DHS—*See* U.S. Department of Homeland Security.

DoC—*See* U.S. Department of Commerce.

DoD—*See* U.S. Department of Defense.

DoDD—*See* Department of Defense Directive.

DoDI—*See* Department of Defense Instruction.

DoS—*See* U.S. Department of State.

DoS and USAID—*See* U.S. Department of Defense and U.S. Agency for International Development.

Dunigan, Molly, Carrie M. Farmer, Rachel M. Burns, Alison Hawks, and Claude Messan Setodji, *Out of the Shadows: The Health and Well-Being of Private Contractors Working in Conflict Environments*, Santa Monica, Calif.: RAND Corporation, RR-420-RC, 2013. As of October 28, 2019: https://www.rand.org/pubs/research_reports/RR420.html

Dunigan, Molly, Michael Schwille, Susanne Sondergaard, Susan S. Sohler Everingham, and Todd Nichols, *Expeditionary Civilians: Creating a Viable Practice of Civilian Deployment Within the U.S. Interagency Community and Among Foreign Defense Organizations*, Santa Monica, Calif.: RAND Corporation, RR-1249-OSD, 2016. As of October 28, 2019: https://www.rand.org/pubs/research_reports/RR1249.html

Dunigan, Molly, Susan S. Sohler Everingham, Todd Nichols, Michael Schwille, and Susanne Sondergaard, *Expeditionary Civilians: Creating a Viable Practice of Department of Defense Civilian Deployment*, Santa Monica, Calif.: RAND Corporation, RR-975-OSD, 2016. As of October 28, 2019:
https://www.rand.org/pubs/research_reports/RR975.html

Elnitsky, Christine A., Michael P. Fisher, and Cara L. Blevins, "Military Service Member and Veteran Reintegration: A Conceptual Analysis, Unified Definition, and Key Domains," *Frontiers in Psychology*, Vol. 8, No. 369, March 14, 2017, pp. 114–128.

Families OverComing Under Stress, "About Us," webpage, undated. As of October 28, 2019:
https://www.focusproject.org/about

Fear, Nicola T., Daniel Meek, Paul Cawkill, Norman Jones, Neil Greenberg, and Simon Wesseley, "The Health of UK Civilians Deployed to Iraq," *European Journal of Public Health*, Vol. 27, No. 2, April 2017, pp. 367–371.

Federal Emergency Management Agency, "About the Agency," webpage, undated. As of October 28, 2019:
https://www.fema.gov/about-agency

Fertout, M., N. Jones, and N. Greenberg. "Third Location Decompression for Individual Augmentees After a Military Deployment," *Occupational Medicine*, Vol. 62, No. 3, April 2012, pp. 188–195.

Field Manual 4-02.51, *Combat and Operational Stress Control*, Washington, D.C.: Headquarters, Department of the Army, July 6, 2006.

Garber, Bryan G., and Mark A. Zamorski, "Evaluation of a Third-Location Decompression Program for Canadian Forces Members Returning From Afghanistan," *Military Medicine*, Vol. 177, No. 4, April 2012, pp. 397–403.

Goldberg, Matthew S., *Updated Death and Injury Rates of U.S. Military Personnel During the Conflicts in Iraq and Afghanistan*, Washington, D.C.: Congressional Budget Office, Working Paper 2014-08, December 2014. As of September 19, 2019:
https://www.cbo.gov/sites/default/files/113th-congress-2013-2014/workingpaper/49837-Casualties_WorkingPaper-2014-08_1.pdf

Goulka, Jeremiah, "It Doesn't Take Much to Get PTSD," *Mother Jones*, April 16, 2013.

Greenleaf Integrative Strategies, *Assessment of Stress and Resilience Issues Affecting USAID Personnel in High Operational Stress Environments*, Washington, D.C.: United States Agency for International Development, September 2015.

Hacker Hughes, Jamie G. H., N. Mark Earnshaw, Neil Greenberg, Rod Eldridge, Nicola T. Fear, Claire French, Martin P. Deahl, and Simon Wessely, "The Use of Psychological Decompression in Military Operational Environments," *Military Medicine,* Vol. 173, No. 6, June 2008, pp. 534–538.

Haga, Barbara, "Employee Participation in Employee Assistance Programs," Federal Employment Law Training Group, undated. As of October 28, 2019: https://feltg.com/employee-participation-in-employee-assistance-programs/

Holloway, Ronald, "Time to Heal and a Place to Thrive," *Foreign Service Journal,* January–February 2016.

Hoskins, Steven, "NECC Hosts Reintegration Training Workshop," U.S. Navy, Navy Expeditionary Combat Command Public Affairs, September 30, 2013. As of October 28, 2019:
http://www.navy.mil/submit/display.asp?story_id=76873

Institute of Medicine, *Returning Home from Iraq and Afghanistan: Assessment of Readjustment Needs of Veterans, Service Members, and Their Families*, Washington, D.C.: National Academies Press, 2013.

Institute of Medicine, *Preventing Psychological Disorder in Service Members and Their Families: An Assessment of Programs*, Washington, D.C.: National Academies Press, 2014.

"Issue Brief: Benefits for Deployed Civilians Vary," *FEDWeek*, August 26, 2009. As of November 4, 2019:
https://www.fedweek.com/issue-briefs/benefits-for-deployed-civilians-vary-2/

Jahnke, Sara, "Rethinking Firefighter Critical-Incident Debriefings," *Fire Rescue News*, October 29, 2015.

Johnson, Kirk, "After the Fall," *Washington Post*, January 28, 2007.

Joint Publication 1-02, *Dictionary of Associated Military Terms*, Washington, D.C.: U.S. Joint Chiefs of Staff, November 8, 2010, as amended through February 15, 2016.

Joyner, James, "Medal Fatigue," *War on the Rocks*, February 3, 2014. As of October 28, 2019:
https://warontherocks.com/2014/02/medal-fatigue/

Lester, Patricia, Li-Jung Liang, Norweeta Milburn, Catherine Mogil, Kirsten Woodward, William Nash, Hilary Aralis, Maegan Sinclair, Alan Semaan, Lee Klosinski, William Beardslee, and William Saltzman, "Evaluation of a Family-Centered Preventive Intervention for Military Families: Parent and Child Longitudinal Outcomes," *Journal of the American Academy of Child and Adolescent Psychiatry*, Vol. 55, No. 1, January 2016, pp. 14–24.

Lynch, Stephen F., "A Call to Arms: A Review of Benefits for Deployed Federal Employees," testimony before the Subcommittee on Federal Workforce, Postal Service, and the District of Columbia, Committee on Oversight and Government Reform, U.S. House of Representatives, Washington, D.C., September 16, 2009.

Macedo, Tania, Livia Wilheim, Raquel Gonçalves, Evandro Silva Freire Coutinho, Liliane Vilete, Ivan Figueira, and Paula Ventura, "Building Resilience for Future Adversity: A Systematic Review of Interventions in Non-Clinical Samples of Adults," *BMC Psychology*, Vol.14, No. 227, 2014.

Management of Posttraumatic Stress Disorder Work Group, *VA/DoD Clinical Practice Guideline for the Management of Posttraumatic Stress Disorder and Acute Stress Disorder*, version 3.0, Washington, D.C.: U.S. Department of Veterans Affairs and U.S. Department of Defense, 2017. As of August 7, 2018: https://www.healthquality.va.gov/guidelines/MH/ptsd/VADoDPTSDCPGFinal012418.pdf

Marek, Lydia I., W. Glenn Hollingsworth, Carissa D'Aniello, Kathleen O'Rourke, Donna-Jean P. Brock, Lyn Moore, John L. Butler VI, Jing Zhang, and Bradford Wiles, "Returning Home: What We Know About the Reintegration of Deployed Service Members into Their Families and Communities," *NCFR Report*, Spring 2012.

Marino, Jennifer L., "Enhancing Resilience Through Post-Deployment Decompression: A Softer Approach to Sharpening the Warrior Edge," master's degree research paper, Marine Corps University, May 2, 2012.

Marine Corps Order 5351.1, *Combat and Operational Stress Control Program*, Department of the Navy, Headquarters, U.S. Marine Corps, February 22, 2013.

McNally, Kyle, "MARSOC: PERRES Continues to Grow," *Tip of the Spear*, February 2013. As of October 28, 2019: https://www.socom.mil/TipOfTheSpear/February%202013%20Tip%20of%20the%20Spear.pdf

Meadows, Sarah O., Terri Tanielian, and Benjamin Karney, eds., *The Deployment Life Study: Longitudinal Analysis of Military Families Across the Deployment Cycle*, Santa Monica, Calif.: RAND Corporation, RR-1388-A/OSD, 2016. As of October 28, 2019: https://www.rand.org/pubs/research_reports/RR1388.html

Meredith, Lisa S., Cathy D. Sherbourne, Sarah J. Gaillot, Lydia Hansell, Hans V. Ritschard, Andrew M. Parker, and Glenda Wrenn, *Promoting Psychological Resilience in the U.S. Military*, Santa Monica, Calif.: RAND Corporation, MG-996-OSD, 2011. As of October 10, 2019: https://www.rand.org/pubs/monographs/MG996.html

Military Health System, "DoD Civilian" webpage, undated. As of January 3, 2020:
https://health.mil/Military-Health-Topics/Health-Readiness/Reserve-Health-Readiness-Program/DoD-Civilian

Mulligan, Kathleen, Nicola T. Fear, Norman Jones, Helen Alvarez, Lisa Hull, Ulrike Naumann, Simon Wessely, and Neil Greenberg, "Battlemind Training for UK Armed Forces: A Cluster Randomised Controlled Trial," *Journal of Consulting and Clinical Psychology*, Vol. 80, No. 3, June 2012, pp. 331–341.

Mulligan, Kathleen, Nicola T. Fear, Norman Jones, Simon Wessely, and Neil Greenberg, "Psycho-Educational Interventions Designed to Prevent Deployment-Related Psychological Ill-Health in Armed Forces Personnel: A Review," *Psychological Medicine*, Vol. 41, No. 4, April 2011, pp. 673–686.

Mulvaney, Mick, "Comprehensive Plan for Reforming the Federal Government and Reducing the Federal Civilian Workforce," memorandum for heads of federal government executive departments and agencies, Washington, D.C.: Executive Office of the President, Office of Management and Budget, April 12, 2017.

Murphy, Patrick, and Mark A. Milley, *A Statement on the Posture of the United States Army 2016*, Washington, D.C.: Department of the Army, March–April 2016.

National Defence and Canadian Forces Ombudsman, *From Tents to Sheets: An Analysis of the CF Experience with Third Location Decompression After Deployment*, Ottawa: Canadian Department of National Defence, 2004.

National Security Presidential Directive NSPD-44, Management of Interagency Efforts Concerning Reconstruction and Stabilization, Washington, D.C.: White House, December 7, 2005.

National Wildlife Coordinating Group, *NWCG Standards for Interagency Incident Business Management*, PMS 902 NFES 002160, March 2016.

Noble, Eric S., and William C. O'Toole, "The Deployment Challenge: Preparing for the Military Deployment and Return of Law Enforcement Officers," *FBI Law Enforcement Bulletin*, Federal Bureau of Investigation, Vol. 78, No. 12, December 2009, pp. 18–24.

Office of the Under Secretary of Defense, Office of Personnel Readiness, *Report to Congress on the 2011 Activities of Force Health Protection Quality Assurance Program of the Department of Defense*, Washington, D.C., November 2012, pp. 43-44.

Office of Workers' Compensation Programs, Division of Federal Employees' Compensation (DFEC), "Information for Deployed Employees and Their Agencies Concerning the Federal Employees' Compensation Act," webpage, U.S. Department of Labor, undated. As of April 20, 2019:
https://www.dol.gov/owcp/dfec/DeployedEmployees.htm

OIE—*See* Office of International Engagement.

OPM—*See* Office of Personnel Management.

Payne, Beth, "Living with Iraq," *Foreign Service Journal*, December 2006, pp. 52–53.

Payne, Beth, "Recovering: When Surviving Isn't Enough," *Foreign Service Journal*, January 2008.

Perito, Robert M., *The U.S. Experience with Provincial Reconstruction Teams in Afghanistan: Lessons Identified*, Special Report 152, Washington, D.C.: United States Institute of Peace, October 2005.

Perito, Robert M., *Provincial Reconstruction Teams in Iraq*, Special Report 185, Washington D.C.: U.S. Institute of Peace, March 2007.

Psychological Health Center of Excellence, "Deployment Health Assessments," webpage, undated. As of October 28, 2019:
http://www.pdhealth.mil/treatment-guidance/deployment-health-assessments

Public Law 112-81, National Defense Authorization Act (NDAA) for Fiscal Year 2012, December 31, 2011.

Public Law 346, Chapter 268, "Servicemen's Readjustment Act of 1944," June 22, 1944.

Ramchand, Rajeev, Reena Rudavsky, Sean Grant, Terri Tanielian, and Lisa Jaycox, "Prevalence of, Risk Factors for, and Consequences of Posttraumatic Stress Disorder and Other Mental Health Problems in Military Populations Deployed to Iraq and Afghanistan," *Current Psychiatry Reports*, Vol. 17, No. 37, May 2015.

Ramstein Air Base, "Air Force Deployment Transition Center," webpage, undated. As of September 20, 2019:
https://www.ramstein.af.mil/Deployment-Transition-Center/

RAND Corporation, "Catalog of Psychological Health and Traumatic Brain Injury Programs," webpage, undated. As of November 7, 2019:
https://smapp.rand.org/multi/military/innovative-practices/catalog/

Rogin, Josh, "Report: 'Stigma' at State Department for Those Seeking Mental Health Treatment," *Washington Post*, August 5, 2010. As of December 27, 2019:
https://www.washingtonpost.com/wp-dyn/content/article/2010/08/04/AR2010080406970.html

Rona, Roberto J., Howard Burdett, Mizanur Khondoker, Melanie Chesnokov, Kevin Green, David Pernet, Norman Jones, Neil Greenberg, Simon Wessely, and Nicola T. Fear, "Post-Deployment Screening for Mental Disorders and Tailored Advice About Help-Seeking in the UK Military: A Cluster Randomised Controlled Trial," *Lancet*, Vol. 389, No. 10077, April 8, 2017, pp. 1410–1423.

Russell, Mark C., and Charles R. Figley, "Do the Military's Frontline Psychiatry/Combat and Operational Stress Control Doctrine Help or Harm Veterans?—Part One: Framing the Issue," *Psychological Injury and Law*, Vol. 10, No. 1, March 2017, pp. 1–23.

Schell, Terry L., Coreen Farris, Jeremy N. V. Miles, Jennifer Sloan, and Deborah M. Scharf, *The Air Force Deployment Transition Center: Assessment of Program Structure, Process, and Outcomes*, Santa Monica, Calif.: RAND Corporation, RR-918-OSD, 2016. As of October 10, 2019:
https://www.rand.org/pubs/research_reports/RR918.html

Schneider, Kristin G., Serena Bezdjian, Danielle Burchett, William C. Isler, David Dickey, and Howard N. Garb, "The Impact of the United States Air Force Deployment Transition Center on Postdeployment Mental Health Outcomes," *Military Psychology*, Vol. 28, No. 2, 2016, pp. 89–103.

Sellers, Cameron S., *Provincial Reconstruction Teams: Improving Effectiveness*, dissertation, Naval Postgraduate School, Monterey, Calif., September 2007.

Sgtbrandi.com, "Caribbean Reintegration Center (CRC) A Mandatory Four Week Combat Decompression Experience. Eleven Months of Deployment, One Month Decompression," webpage, March 3, 2008. As of October 28, 2019:
http://sgtbrandi.com/?page_id=2015

"Talking Paper on Deployment Transition Center," Ramstein Air Base, August 2015.

Thielman, Samuel B., "Help After High-Stress Assignments," *Foreign Service Journal*, 2006.

Thomas, Harry K., "Civilians on the Battlefield: Incentives, Benefits and Medical Care for Federal Civilian Employees Deployed to Iraq and Afghanistan," testimony before the House Armed Services Committee, Subcommittee on Oversight and Investigations, October 16, 2007.

Trail, Thomas E., Laurie T. Martin, Lane F. Burgette, Linnea Warren May, Ammarah Mahmud, Nupur Nanda, and Anita Chandra, *An Evaluation of U.S. Military Non-Medical Counseling Programs*, Santa Monica, Calif.: RAND Corporation, RR-1861-OSD, 2017. As of November 7, 2019:
https://www.rand.org/pubs/research_reports/RR1861.html

Transportation Security Administration, "About," webpage, undated. As of October 28, 2019:
https://www.tsa.gov/about

United Kingdom Ministry of Defence, "Preparing Civilian Staff for Operational Deployments," September 14, 2012. As of October 28, 2019:
https://www.gov.uk/government/news/preparing-civilian-staff-for-operational-deployments

U.S. Agency for International Development, "About the ADS," webpage, last updated October 28, 2013. As of May 19, 2019:
https://www.usaid.gov/who-we-are/agency-policy/about-ads

U.S. Agency for International Development, "ADS Series 400," webpage, last updated September 24, 2019a. As of May 19, 2019:
https://www.usaid.gov/who-we-are/agency-policy/series-400

U.S. Agency for International Development, "Staff Care," webpage, last updated September 17, 2019b. As of November 11, 2019:
https://staffcare.usaid.gov/services.html

U.S. Agency for International Development, Chapter 436, Foreign Service Assignments and Tours of Duty, *Automated Directives System*, October 18, 2011. As of November 11, 2019:
https://www.usaid.gov/sites/default/files/documents/1877/436.pdf

U.S. Agency for International Development, "Staffing Report to Congress," June 2016.

U.S. Agency for International Development, "Mission, Visions, Values," webpage, last updated February 16, 2018. As of November 11, 2019:
https://www.usaid.gov/who-we-are/mission-vision-values

U.S. Agency for International Development, "Office of U.S. Foreign Disaster Assistance," webpage, last updated May 7, 2019a. As of December 12, 2019:
https://www.usaid.gov/who-we-are/organization/bureaus/bureau-democracy-conflict-and-humanitarian-assistance/office-us

U.S. Agency for International Development, "What We Do," webpage, last updated August 22, 2019b. As of November 11, 2019:
https://www.usaid.gov/what-we-do

USAID—*See* U.S. Agency for International Development.

U.S. Air Force, Deployment Transition Center, "Comprehensive Airman Fitness Brochure," September 2018.

U.S. Army Europe, "USAREUR Reintegration Model," October 29, 2003.

U.S. Army, Human Resources Command, "The Adjutant General Directorate (TAGD): PERSTEMPO FAQs," webpage, last updated November 25, 2019. As of October 28, 2019:
https://www.hrc.army.mil/content/PERSTEMPO%20FAQs

U.S. Citizenship and Immigration Services, *USCIS Strategic Plan FY 2017–2021*, Washington D.C.: U.S. Department of Homeland Security, November 16, 2016. As of November 11, 2019:
https://www.uscis.gov/sites/default/files/USCIS/About%20Us/Budget%2C%20Planning%20and%20Performance/USCIS_2017-2021_Strategic_Plan.pdf

U.S. Citizenship and Immigration Services, "About Us," webpage, last updated March 6, 2018. As of October 28, 2019:
https://www.uscis.gov/aboutus

U.S. Code, Title 5, Government Organization and Employees, Section 2101, Civil Service; Armed Forces; Uniformed Services.

U.S. Code, Title 5, Government Organization and Employees, Section 7901, Health Service Programs.

U.S. Code, Title 5, Government Organization and Employees, Section 7906, Services of Post-Combat Case Coordinators.

U.S. Code, Title 5, Government Organization and Employees, Section 8101, Definitions.

U.S. Code, Title 22, Foreign Service and Intercourse, Chapter 52, Foreign Service.

U.S. Code, Title 22, Foreign Relations and Intercourse, Section 3902, Definitions.

U.S. Code, Title 31, Money and Finance, Section 1535, Agency Agreements.

U.S. Code, Title 48, Federal Acquisition Regulations System, Section 37.104, Personal Services Contracts.

U.S. Customs and Border Protection, "About CBP," webpage, last modified September 18, 2019a. As of October 28, 2019:
https://www.cbp.gov/about

U.S. Customs and Border Protection, "Careers," webpage, last modified November 21, 2019b. As of November 11, 2019:
https://www.cbp.gov/careers

U.S. Department of the Air Force, *Post Deployment Processing Checklist (Military Personnel)*, August 2005.

U.S. Department of the Air Force, *Deployment Planning And Execution*, Air Force Instruction 10-403, September 20, 2012.

U.S. Department of the Air Force, *Disaster Mental Health Response & Combat and Operational Stress Control*, Air Force Instruction 44-153, May 29, 2014a.

U.S. Department of the Air Force, *Airman and Family Readiness Centers*, Air Force Instruction 36-3009, July 16, 2014b.

U.S. Department of the Air Force, *Deployment Health*, Air Force Instruction 48-122, August 18, 2014c.

U.S. Department of the Air Force, *Absence and Leave*, Air Force Instruction 36-825, July 8, 2015.

U.S. Department of the Air Force, *Awards and Decoration Program*, Air Force Policy Directive 36-28, April 26, 2016a.

U.S. Department of the Air Force, *Military Leave Policy*, Air Force Instruction 36-3003, May 11, 2016b.

U.S. Department of Agriculture, U.S. Forest Service, "About the Agency," webpage, undated. As of December 13, 2017:
https://www.fs.fed.us/about-agency

U.S. Department of Agriculture, U.S. Forest Service, *Fiscal Year 2017 Budget Overview*, Washington, D.C., February 2016. As of November 11, 2019:
https://www.fs.fed.us/sites/default/files/fy-2017-fs-budget-overview.pdf

U.S. Department of the Army, "Department of the Army Civilian Post-Deployment Health Reassessment Implementation Guidance," Washington, D.C., memorandum, undated.

U.S. Department of the Army, *DA Civilian Employee Deployment Guide*, Pamphlet 690-47, November 1, 1995.

U.S. Department of the Army, *Department of the Army Global War on Terrorism (GWOT) Post Conflict/Mobilization Personnel Operations*, Deployment Cycle Support (DCS) Concept Plan (CONPLAN), May 2, 2003a. As of January 3, 2019:
https://ssilrc.army.mil/wp-content/uploads/2017/03/ALC_DCS_CONPLAN.pdf

U.S. Department of the Army, *Personnel Processing (In-, Out-, Soldier Readiness, Mobilization, and Deployment Processing)*, Army Regulation 600-8-101, July 18, 2003b.

U.S. Department of the Army, *Department of the Army Personnel Policy Guidance for Overseas Contingency Operations*, periodic review dated July 1, 2009.

U.S. Department of the Army, *Personnel Recovery*, Army Regulation 525-28, March 2010a.

U.S. Department of the Army, *Installation Clearance Record*, DA Form 137-2, June 2010b.

U.S. Department of the Army, "PHDRA Frequently Asked Questions," 2011a. As of December 12, 2017:
http://www.armyg1.army.mil/hr/pdhra/docs/PDHRA_FAQ_2011.pdf

U.S. Department of the Army, *Leaves and Passes*, Army Regulation 600-8-10, August 4, 2011b.

U.S. Department of the Army, *Army Personnel Policy Guidance*, August 2013.

U.S. Department of the Army, *Comprehensive Soldier and Family Fitness*, Army Regulation 350-53, June 19, 2014a.

U.S. Department of the Army, "GAT 2.0 for Spouses," webpage, July 14, 2014b. As of January 3, 2020:
https://www.army.mil/standto/2014-07-14

U.S. Department of the Army, *Unit Clearance Record*, DA Form 137-1, February 2015a.

U.S. Department of the Army, *Personnel Accounting and Strength Reporting*, Army Regulation 600-8-6, April 1, 2015b.

U.S. Department of the Army, *Military Awards*, Army Regulation 600-8-22, June 25, 2015c.

U.S. Department of Army, U.S. Army Corps of Engineers, *USACE Deployment Handbook for USACE Personnel and Family Members*, December 2009.

U.S. Department of Commerce, "About Commerce," webpage, undated. As of November 11, 2019:
https://www.commerce.gov/about

U.S. Department of Commerce, *U.S. Department of Commerce Strategic Plan, FY 2011–2016*, Washington, D.C., 2011. As of November 11, 2019:
http://www.osec.doc.gov/bmi/budget/DOCFY11-16StrategicPlan%20_508version.pdf

U.S. Department of Defense, "Privacy Impact Assessment (PIA) for the Personnel Tempo (PERSTEMPO) Department of the Navy, Bureau of Naval Personnel (BUPERS)," DD Form 2930, November 2008.

U.S. Department of Defense, *Military Deployment Guide*, updated February 2012a.

U.S. Department of Defense, "Pre-Deployment Health Assessment," DD Form 2795, September 2012b.

U.S. Department of Defense, *Report to the Congressional Defense Committees in Response to Section 702 of the National Defense Authorization Act for Fiscal Year 2012 (Public Law 112-81): Mental Health Assessments for Members of the Armed Forces Deployed in Support of a Contingency Operation*, Washington, D.C., July 30, 2013.

U.S. Department of Defense, "Deployment Mental Health Assessment," DD Form 2978, February 2014.

U.S. Department of Defense, "Post Deployment Health Assessment (PDHA)," DD Form 2796, October 2015a.

U.S. Department of Defense, "Post-Deployment Health Re-Assessment (PDHRA)," DD Form 2900, October 2015b.

U.S. Department of Health and Human Services, Program Support Center, Federal Occupational Health, "About FOH," webpage, undated-a. As of October 28, 2019:
https://foh.psc.gov/about.html

U.S. Department of Health and Human Services, Program Support Center, Federal Occupational Health "Doing Business with FOH and Interagency Agreements (IAAs)," webpage, undated-b. As of October 28, 2019: https://foh.psc.gov/about/agreements.html

U.S. Department of Health and Human Services, Federal Occupational Health, "Employee Assistance Program," webpage, undated-a. As of November 11, 2019: https://foh.psc.gov/public/factsheets/eap.pdf

U.S. Department of Health and Human Services, Federal Occupational Health, "The Interagency Agreement," webpage, undated-b. As of November 11, 2019: https://foh.psc.gov/public/interagency.pdf

U.S. Department of Homeland Security, "The Office of International Engagement," webpage, last updated August 31, 2017. As of November 11, 2019: https://www.dhs.gov/office-international-affairs

U.S. Department of Homeland Security, *Federal Emergency Management Agency: Budget Overview, Fiscal Year 2018 Congressional Justification*, Washington, D.C., 2018. As of October 28, 2019: https://www.dhs.gov/sites/default/files/publications/FEMA%20FY18%20Budget.pdf

U.S. Department of Homeland Security, Office of Strategy, Policy, and Plans, "Office of International Engagement," webpage, undated. As of October 28, 2019: https://www.dhs.gov/office-international-engagement

U.S. Department of Justice, "Drug Enforcement Administration (DEA)," fact sheet, 2017. As of November 11, 2019: https://www.justice.gov/jmd/file/822096/download

U.S. Department of the Navy, *Naval Military Personnel Manual*, Millington, Tenn., NAVPERS 15560D, August 22, 2002.

U.S. Department of the Navy, Office of the Chief Naval Officer, "Combat and Operational Stress Control and Warrior Transition Program Administration," memorandum, NAVADMIN 182/07, July 23, 2007.

U.S. Department of the Navy, U.S. Marine Corps, "Combat Operational Stress Control (COSC) Program," Marine Corps Bulletin 6490, September 18, 2008.

U.S. Department of the Navy, "Command Return, Reunion, and Reintegration (R3) Program Standard Operating Procedure (SOP)," memorandum from Parent Command, August 2011. As of November 11, 2019: https://www.public.navy.mil/IA/Documents/R3SOPTempAug2011.pdf

U.S. Department of the Navy, *Redeployment and Demobilization Administrative Screening Checklist*, NAVPERS 1300/23, August 2012.

U.S. Department of the Navy, *Headquarters Personnel Check-in/Check-Out and Orientation Procedures*, CNIC Instruction 5300.4A, February 12, 2013a.

U.S. Department of the Navy, *Leave Policy*, MILPERSMAN 1050-10, March 29, 2013b.

U.S. Department of the Navy, *Navy Personnel Tempo and Operating Tempo Program*, OPNAVINST 300.13D, March 14, 2014a.

U.S. Department of the Navy, *Deployment Health Assessment Process*, OPNAVINST 6100.3A, November 10, 2014b.

U.S. Department of the Navy, *Operational Stress Control Program*, OPNAVINST 6520.1, June 24, 2015.

U.S. Department of the Navy, *Military Awards Guidance*, NAVPERSCOM Instruction 1650.3D, April 19, 2016.

U.S. Department of the Navy, U.S. Fleet Forces Command, "Navy Individual Augmentee: Navy IA Messages and Policy," *Navy Individual Augmentee,* webpage, undated-a. As of November 4, 2019:
https://www.public.navy.mil/ia/Pages/PD_PC_POLICY.aspx

U.S. Department of the Navy, U.S. Fleet Forces Command, "Return, Reintegration, and Re-Deployment (R3)," *Navy Individual Augmentee*, webpage, undated-b. As of November 4, 2019:
https://www.public.navy.mil/ia/Pages/R3.aspx

U.S. Department of the Navy, U.S. Marine Corps, *Combat and Operational Stress Control*, NTTP 1-15M, MCRP 6-11C, Washington, D.C., December 2010.

U.S. Department of the Navy, U.S. Marine Corps, *Operational Stress Control and Readiness Training Guidance*, MARADMIN 597/11, October 7, 2011.

U.S. Department of State, "Domestic/Civil Service," webpage, undated-a. As of November 11, 2019:
https://careers.state.gov/work/civil-service/

U.S. Department of State, "Foreign Service Officer," webpage, undated-b. As of November 11, 2019:
https://careers.state.gov/work/foreign-service/officer/

U.S. Department of State, "Going Home: Re-Adapting Can Be Difficult," brochure, undated-c.

U.S. Department of State, "High Stress Assignment Outbrief Program," webpage, undated-d. As of October 28, 2019:
https://2009-2017.state.gov/m/fsi/tc/hsaop//index.htm

U.S. Department of State, "Definitions," *Foreign Affairs Manual*, Vol. 3, Chapter 3342, July 28, 2015.

U.S. Department of State, *Agency Financial Report, Fiscal Year 2016*, Washington, D.C.: U.S. Department of State, Bureau of Public Affairs, November 2016.

U.S. Department of State, "Personal Services Contractors (PSC)," *Foreign Affairs Manual*, Vol. 3, Chapter 9000, 2017a.

U.S. Department of State, *Congressional Budget Justification: Department of State, Foreign Operations, and Related Programs, Fiscal Year 2018*, Washington, D.C., May 23, 2017b.

U.S. Department of State, "Rest and Recuperation (R&R) Travel," *Foreign Affairs Manual*, Vol. 3, Chapter 3720, September 2018. As of December 17, 2019: https://fam.state.gov/FAM/03FAM/03FAM3720.html

U.S. Department of State, "Deployment Stress Management Program (DSMP)," *Foreign Affairs Manual*, Vol. 16, Chapter 440, March 2019a. As of December 17, 2019:
https://fam.state.gov/searchapps/viewer?format=html&query=Vol.%2016,%20Chapter%20440,&links=16,440&url=/FAM/16FAM/16FAM0440.html

U.S. Department of State, "Purpose," *Foreign Affairs Manual*, Vol. 16, Chapter 441, March 2019b.

U.S. Department of State, "Shared Voluntary Leave Programs," *Foreign Affairs Handbook*, Vol. 3, Chapter 3340, October 2019c.

U.S. Department of State, Broadcasting Board of Governors, Office of Inspector General, *Report of Inspection: Review of Support for Employees Who Are Serving or Have Served in High Stress, High Threat, Unaccompanied Posts*, Washington, D.C., Report No. ISP-I-10-44, July 2010. As of December 17, 2018:
https://oig.state.gov/system/files/145424.pdf

U.S. Department of State, Foreign Service Institute, "Personal Resilience Action Plan," handout, undated.

U.S. Department of State, Office of Inspector General, homepage, undated. As of January 12, 2018:
https://www.stateoig.gov

U.S. Department of State, Bureau of Medical Services, "Key Topics: Deployment Stress Management Program," webpage, undated. As of November 11, 2019:
https://www.state.gov/key-topics-deployment-stress-management-program/

U.S. Department of State and U.S. Agency for International Development, *Enduring Leadership in a Dynamic World: Quadrennial Diplomacy and Development Review*, Washington, D.C., 2015. As of October 28, 2019:
https://www.usaid.gov/sites/default/files/documents/1870/QDDR2015.pdf

U.S. Department of Treasury, "Role of the Treasury," webpage, undated. As of October 28, 2019:
https://home.treasury.gov/about/general-information/role-of-the-treasury

U.S. Department of Treasury, "FY 2018, Executive Summary: Congressional Justification For Appropriations And Annual Performance Report And Plan," 2018. As of November 11, 2019:
https://www.treasury.gov/about/budget-performance/CJ18/02%20-%2004.%20Executive%20Summary.pdf

U.S. Department of Veterans Affairs, "PTSD: National Center for PTSD, Types of Debriefing Following Disasters," webpage, last updated February 23, 2016. As of October 28, 2019:
https://www.ptsd.va.gov/professional/treat/type/debrief_after_disasters.asp

U.S. Drug Enforcement Administration, "Mission: DEA Mission Statement," webpage, undated. As of November 11, 2019:
https://www.dea.gov/mission

U.S. Government Accountability Office, *Provincial Reconstruction Teams in Afghanistan and Iraq*, Washington, D.C., GAO-09-86R, October 1, 2008.

U.S. House of Representatives, Committee on Armed Services, Subcommittee on Oversight and Investigations, *Deploying Federal Civilians to the Battlefield: Incentives, Benefits, and Medical Care,* Washington, D.C., April 2008. As of January 17, 2018:
https://democrats-armedservices.house.gov/_cache/files/4/1/41c00ebb-a344-4666-afe3-210eac7680f5/1EC4601C51CE23B55D117C87EF15A284.civilians-on-battlefield-report-vf.pdf

U.S. Immigration and Customs Enforcement, *Strategic Plan: 2016–2020*, Washington, D.C.: U.S. Department of Homeland Security, January 2016.

U.S. Immigration and Customs Enforcement, "What We Do," webpage, last updated December 4, 2018. As of November 11, 2019:
https://www.ice.gov/overview

U.S. Immigration and Customs Enforcement, "History," webpage, last updated March 4, 2019. As of November 11, 2019:
https://www.ice.gov/history

U.S. Joint Forces Command Joint Warfighting Center, "Provincial Reconstruction Teams," pre-doctrinal research white paper No. 07-01, November 21, 2007.

U.S. Office of Personnel Management, "Data, Analysis and Documentation," webpage, undated-a. As of November 11, 2019:
https://www.opm.gov/policy-data-oversight/data-analysis-documentation/

U.S. Office of Personnel Management, "FedScope: Federal Workforce Data," webpage, undated-b. As of August 5, 2017:
https://www.fedscope.opm.gov/

U.S. Office of Personnel Management, "Pay & Leave: Leave Administration," webpage, undated-c. As of November 11, 2019:
https://www.opm.gov/policy-data-oversight/pay-leave/leave-administration/fact-sheets/annual-leave/

U.S. Office of Personnel Management, "What Is an Employee Assistance Program (EAP)?" webpage, undated-d. As of November 11, 2019:
https://www.opm.gov/faqs/QA.aspx?fid=4313c618-a96e-4c8e-b078-1f76912a10d9&pid=2c2b1e5b-6ff1-4940-b478-34039a1e1174

U.S. Office of Personnel Management, *Federal Employee Assistance Programs: Guiding Principles, Framework, and Definitions*, Washington, D.C., September 2008.

U.S. Office of Personnel Management, "Guidelines: Post-Combat Case Coordinator," BAL 13-201, Washington, D.C., 2013. As of December 17, 2019: https://www.opm.gov/retirement-services/publications-forms/benefits-administration-letters/2013/13-201attachment1.pdf

Vaughan, Christine Anne, Carrie M. Farmer, Joshua Breslau, and Crystal Burnette, *Evaluation of the Operational Stress Control and Readiness (OSCAR) Program*, Santa Monica, Calif.: RAND Corporation, RR-562-OSD, 2015. As of October 10, 2019:
https://www.rand.org/pubs/research_reports/RR562.html

Vermetten, Eric, Neil Greenberg, Manon A. Boeschoten, Roos Delahaije, Rakesh Jetly, Carl A. Castro, and Alexander C. McFarlane, "Deployment-Related Mental Health Support: Comparative Analysis of NATO and Allied ISAF Partners," *European Journal of Psychotraumatology*, Vol. 5, No. 1, 2014.

Warner, Christopher H., George N. Appenzeller, Jessica R. Parker, Carolynn M. Warner, and Charles W. Hoge, "Effectiveness of Mental Health Screening and Coordination of In-Theater Care Prior to Deployment to Iraq: A Cohort Study," *American Journal of Psychiatry*, Vol. 168, No. 4, April 2011, pp. 378–385.

Warner, Christopher H., George N. Appenzeller, Thomas Grieger, Slava Belenkiy, Jill Brietbach, Jessica R. Parker, Carolynn M. Warner, and Charles W. Hoge, "Importance of Anonymity to Encourage Honest Reporting in Mental Health Screening After Combat Deployment," *Archives of General Psychiatry*, Vol. 68, No. 10, October 2011, pp. 1065–1071.

Weinick, Robin M., Ellen Burke Beckjord, Carrie M. Farmer, Laurie T. Martin, Emily M. Gillen, Joie D. Acosta, Michael P. Fisher, Jeffrey Garnett, Gabriella C. Gonzalez, Todd C. Helmus, Lisa H. Jaycox, Kerry Reynolds, Nicholas Salcedo, and Deborah M. Scharf, *Programs Addressing Psychological Health and Traumatic Brain Injury Among U.S. Military Servicemembers and Their Families*, Santa Monica, Calif.: RAND Corporation, TR-950-OSD, 2011. As of October 27, 2019: https://www.rand.org/pubs/technical_reports/TR950.html

Werber, Laura, Jennie W. Wenger, Agnes Gereben Schaefer, Lindsay Daugherty, and Mollie Rudnick, *An Assessment of Fiscal Year 2013 Beyond Yellow Ribbon Programs*, Santa Monica, Calif.: RAND Corporation, RR-965-OSD, 2015. As of October 10, 2019:
https://www.rand.org/pubs/research_reports/RR965.html

Werber, Laura, Kathryn Pitkin Derose, Mollie Rudnick, Margaret C. Harrell, and Diana Naranjo, *Faith-Based Organizations and Veteran Reintegration: Enriching the Web of Support*, Santa Monica, Calif.: RAND Corporation, RR-931-RC, 2015. As of October 10, 2019:
https://www.rand.org/pubs/research_reports/RR931.html

Werber, Laura, Agnes Gereben Schaefer, Karen Chan Osilla, Elizabeth Wilke, Anny Wong, Joshua Breslau, and Karin E. Kitchens, *Support for the 21st-Century Reserve Force: Insights to Facilitate Successful Reintegration for Citizen Warriors and Their Families*, Santa Monica, Calif.: RAND Corporation, RR-206-OSD, 2013. As of October 27, 2019:
https://www.rand.org/pubs/research_reports/RR206.html

Whybrow, Dean, Norman Jones, and Neil Greenberg, "Promoting Organizational Well-Being: A Comprehensive Review of Trauma Risk Management," *Occupational Medicine*, Vol. 65, No. 4, June 2015, pp. 331–336.

Wilcox, Amanda, "Marine Corps Sending Most Elite to 'Special' Decompression, Psychological Screening Center After War Duty," *Jacksonville Daily News*, August 29, 2012.

Wilcox, Sherrie L., Hyunsung Oh, Sarah A. Redmond, Joseph Chicas, Anthony M. Hassan, Pey-Jiuan Lee, and Kathleen Ell, "A Scope of the Problem: Post-Deployment Reintegration Challenges in a National Guard Unit," *Work*, Vol. 50, No. 1, 2015, pp. 73–83.

Wright, Robin, "Stress Taking Toll on Foreign Service," *Washington Post*, June 20, 2007.

Yosick, Todd, Mark Bates, Monique Moore, Chris Crowe, Jennifer Phillips, and John Davison, *A Review of Post-Deployment Reintegration: Evidence, Challenges, and Strategies for Program Development*, Arlington, Va.: Defense Centers of Excellence for Psychological Health and Traumatic Brain Injury, February 2012.

Zamorski, Mark A., and Bryan G. Garber, "Drivers of the Perceived Value of a Third-Location Decompression Program for Canadian Forces Personnel Returning From Afghanistan," *Military Behavioral Health*, Vol. 1, No. 1, 2013, pp. 4–12.

Zamorski, Mark A., Kim Guest, Suzanne Bailey, and Bryan G. Garber, "Beyond Battlemind: Evaluation of a New Mental Health Training Program for Canadian Forces Personnel Participating in Third-Location Decompression," *Military Medicine*, Vol. 177, No. 11, November 2012, pp. 1245–1253.

Zoroya, Gregg, "Wildfire Crews Battle PTSD, Much Like Soldiers at War," *USA Today*, September 6, 2014.

About the Authors

Molly Dunigan is a senior political scientist and associate director of the Defense and Political Sciences department at the RAND Corporation, and a lecturer in Carnegie Mellon University's Institute for Politics and Strategy. Her research interests focus on private military and security contractors, civil–military relations, irregular warfare, counterinsurgency, maritime security, and civilian deployment. She is the recipient of numerous awards, including a U.S. Institute of Peace Jennings Randolph Peace Fellowship, a U.S. State Department Foreign Language Areas Studies Fellowship, and an International Studies Association Catalytic Research Grant.

Kristie L. Gore is a senior behavioral scientist at the RAND Corporation. Her research expertise includes applying health services approaches to the prevention and treatment of behavioral health conditions. Her recent research includes: an evaluation of the prevalence of sexual assault in service members, the development of a survey to assess racial and ethnic harassment and discrimination in the military, a randomized clinical trial to help the spouses of service members who are abusing alcohol, and a strategic planning effort to develop a prioritized research agenda on psychological health and traumatic brain injury. Gore served as the associate director in the Forces and Resources Policy Center in the National Security Research Division from 2013 to 2018. In that role she managed the military health studies portfolio, primarily serving the Office of the Secretary of Defense.

Katherine L. Kidder is an associate political scientist at the RAND Corporation. Her research specializations include Department of Defense institutional and organizational design and management; military recruitment, retention, and talent management policy; professional military education; military readiness; and ground force concept development. Her current research includes an evaluation of Defense Officer Personnel Management Act modernization efforts; the role of service culture in generating flag and general officers; and an examination of potential leading indicators that may assist the Department of Defense in preventing Class A accidents.

Michael Schwille is a senior policy analyst at the RAND Corporation, where he focuses on issues related to operations in the information environment, force modernization, concept development and personnel management. Prior to joining RAND, he worked at the Defense Intelligence Agency and worked in the international development field. He has been in the U.S. Army for 15 years, serving as a Civil Affairs and Psychological Operations Officer.

Samantha Cherney is a quantitative analyst at the RAND Corporation. Her research portfolio includes work on civil and criminal justice, insurance, and army contracting, and on the Gun Policy in America initiative.

James Sladden, formerly a policy analyst at the RAND Corporation researching Europe, Russia, and the Middle East, is currently a Deployable Civilian Expert with the Stabilisation Unit, a UK cross-government agency.